How to Revise
for GCSE

Become the ultimate revision machine with CGP!

At CGP, we're revision experts. We even built a robot that just did revision 24 hours a day, but it went a bit haywire and blew up our coffee machine. We had to take its batteries out.

That taught us not to mess with robots, but we can still turn you into a 100% efficient GCSE revision device. That's why we've made this book — it's packed with failsafe CGP study techniques that'll make sure you've <u>really</u> learned everything you need for the exams.

And with ultra-helpful checklists, timetables and planners included, you can cruise calmly through your revision without any unfortunate explosions. Unlike poor old Revise-O-Tron...

How to access your free Online Edition

This book includes a free Online Edition to read on your PC, Mac or tablet.
You'll just need to go to **cgpbooks.co.uk/extras** and enter this code:

3539 8039 7745 6635

By the way, this code only works for one person. If somebody else has used
this book before you, they might have already claimed the Online Edition.

Contents

Published by CGP

Editors:
Tom Carney, Andy Cashmore, Heather Cowley, Gabrielle Richardson, Matt Topping

Contributors:
Ben Armstrong, Graham Fletcher, Steve Gough, David Martindill, Deanne Morris, Steve Stoddard, Sue Todd, Ben Wallace

With thanks to Holly Robinson and Elisabeth Quincey for the proofreading.
With thanks to Emily Smith for the copyright research.

ISBN: 978 1 78908 280 7

Printed by Elanders Ltd, Newcastle upon Tyne.

Clipart from Corel®
Based on the classic CGP style created by Richard Parsons.

How To Use This Book

It's hard to know where to start with revision, but like a good blanket this book has you covered. Below you'll find all the goodness contained within these pages that will help make your revision less daunting.

Read the *First Half* for *Revision Advice*

The first half of this book gives you guidance and strategies on how best to revise:

Making a Start

This section gives you general advice on how to get yourself ready to revise.

Revision Techniques

This section gives you plenty of ideas for different ways to revise.

Get to Know the Exams

You'll learn all about what to expect in your exams in this section — this will help you get ready for them in your revision.

Know Your Subject

The fourth section gives you subject-specific revision techniques.

On The Day

The last section talks you through how to prepare and cope with exam day.

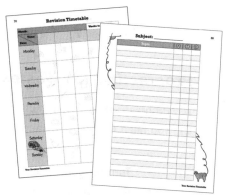

Use the *Second Half* to Plan Your Revision

1) At the back of this book are an exam timetable, topic planners and revision timetables for you to fill in.
2) There's also step-by-step information on how to plan your revision so you use your time wisely.
3) Once you've read the book and filled in your revision timetable, you'll be all set to start revising.

Go forth brave adventurer — your revision journey is about to begin...

Revision is difficult, but to get on top of it you have to put the effort in. Becoming the greatest reviser in the land requires dedicating time to learning the best ways to revise — oh and this book, don't forget this book...

Motivation and Procrastination

Let's address the elephant in the book — you'd probably rather be doing anything other than revising (even reading about how to revise). But thinking about how revision can help with your future goals may (hear me out) make it seem less terrible.

Knowing Why You're Revising Can Motivate You

1) Think about <u>why</u> you want to do well in your exams. It may be:
   - to get into a good <u>sixth form</u> or <u>college</u> after your GCSEs
   - to help you one day get your <u>dream job</u>
   - to <u>prove to yourself</u> and others that you can do it

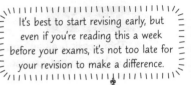
It's best to start revising early, but even if you're reading this a week before your exams, it's not too late for your revision to make a difference.

2) Whatever your goal, it's best to <u>start</u> revising as <u>soon as possible</u>.

3) Be <u>positive</u> about revision — it can be tough, but it'll <u>really help</u> when exams arrive.

4) Focus on <u>your goals</u> and <u>don't compare</u> yourself to other people.

Five <u>Top Tips</u> For Staying Motivated

1. Set <u>small targets</u> with <u>rewards</u> (see p.4).
2. Remind yourself of your <u>long-term goals</u>.
3. Plan a <u>big treat</u> for <u>after your exams</u>.
4. Use a <u>topic planner</u> so you can see the <u>progress</u> you've made.
5. If you're <u>dreading</u> a particular topic, start with some <u>easier topics first</u>.

Procrastination Wastes Valuable Time

1) Procrastination means <u>putting off a task</u> that needs doing.

2) You need to <u>avoid procrastination</u> to make the most of your revision:

This climb takes the biscuit...

- Turn off your <u>phone</u>, <u>television</u> and other distractions.
- Give yourself <u>regular breaks</u> — it'll help you keep <u>focused</u> when you're revising.
- Break up your revision into <u>small chunks</u> so it's not one endless slog.
- <u>Start</u> with something <u>small</u> — this will ease you into focusing on your work.

Organisation and Planning

Some things are best when you dive straight in — revision is not one of those things. Making a plan means you can spend more time revising and less time worrying you've forgotten something.

Planning Will Make You Feel in Control

Spend time on a solid revision plan, but don't spend so long that you don't have time to revise.

Reasons to Plan

* You know you <u>have time</u> to <u>cover everything</u>
* You <u>won't forget</u> any topics
* You can <u>prioritise</u> early exams or tricky subjects
* It <u>reduces stress</u>
* It's <u>more efficient</u>

What Happens Without a Plan

* You'll <u>waste time</u> deciding what to revise each session
* You might <u>not</u> allow <u>enough time</u> to revise everything
* You <u>can't easily check</u> what you've already revised
* You may <u>forget</u> some topics

Timetables Can Help You Plan Your Revision

A revision timetable and topic planner will help you schedule your revision and see how you're progressing. You can find handy versions ready to fill in at the back of this book on pages 53-85.

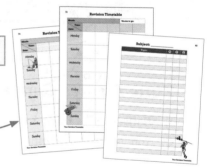

Being Organised Will Save Time

1) Organise your <u>notes and books</u> for each subject to make it easier to <u>find information</u>.

2) Write a <u>to-do list</u>, then <u>prioritise</u> which tasks need to be done first.

3) Make sure you have all the <u>stationery you need</u> (lots of paper, pens, a calculator etc.) so you can crack on with your revision without a fuss.

To-Do List

1 • Buy pens and a new protractor ✓
3 • Tidy desk ✓
2 • Organise Physics notes folder ✓
4 • Clean boots for rugby practice ✓
5 • Write the most hilarious, side-splitting joke to round off the 'Organisation and Planning' page.

Did you hear the one about

Planning your revision will help you remember to get every little last thing done. Eventually...

Setting Targets

Knowing what you want to achieve in each revision session is important — it keeps you on track.

Make Targets Small and Realistic

EXAMPLE:

Imagine you are revising GCSE History. Here's how you could set targets for your revision session.

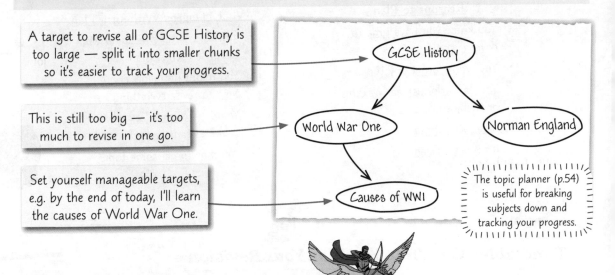

A target to revise all of GCSE History is too large — split it into smaller chunks so it's easier to track your progress.

This is still too big — it's too much to revise in one go.

Set yourself manageable targets, e.g. by the end of today, I'll learn the causes of World War One.

GCSE History

World War One

Norman England

Causes of WWI

The topic planner (p.54) is useful for breaking subjects down and tracking your progress.

Time Frames Can Help You to be Efficient

1) Setting a time frame to achieve your targets helps with <u>motivation</u>.

2) You need to be <u>realistic</u> though. For example:

- Two weeks for fractions — this is <u>too long</u> on a <u>small topic</u>.
- An hour for all of chemistry — you'll either have <u>too little time</u> or <u>rush</u> through it.

3) Generally, it's better to give yourself <u>slightly more</u> time than you think you'll need.

Reward Yourself For Hitting Targets

1) An incentive could <u>encourage</u> you to work hard to hit your targets.

2) You might plan a reward for finishing a <u>tricky topic</u> or doing a <u>practice paper</u>.

3) Your rewards should be <u>simple</u> and <u>help you relax</u> — e.g. some TV or a walk.

4) Plan a <u>large treat</u> for after your exams as something to <u>look forward</u> to.

Your Revision Environment

To be productive, it's important to know what environment you revise best in. For example, that gymnast in your class may find it easier to work in a completely different way to you...

Different Places *Work Best for Different People*

There's no one right place to revise. Based on how you <u>work best</u>, you'll find some places make you feel <u>more productive</u> than others:

Library

✓ Lots of <u>books</u> about subjects you're revising

✓ Access to the <u>internet</u> for research

✓ <u>Fewer distractions</u> than at home or with friends

✗ It may be <u>busy</u> and hard to get a desk

✗ It can involve time <u>spent travelling</u>

Bedroom At Home

✓ You can <u>set up</u> your <u>study space</u> as you want

✓ You can shut yourself away for <u>privacy</u>

✓ It's easy to get <u>healthy snacks</u> and <u>drinks</u>

✗ You may get <u>distracted</u> by your <u>family</u>

✗ <u>Television</u> and <u>games</u> are easy to find

Friend's House

✓ You can <u>discuss revision</u> problems with your friend

✓ You and your friend can <u>test</u> each other

✗ You and your friend could <u>distract</u> each other

✗ You may become <u>disheartened</u> or <u>stressed</u> if your friend seems to know more than you

A Tidy Study Space *is Important*

You'll find it <u>easier to revise</u> if your study space is <u>free of clutter</u>. Here's one we made earlier:

Door closed to shut out any noise

A panda, obviously

Stationery neat and nearby

Well-lit space — easy to read

No distractions — TV unplugged, phone off and not on study desk

Tidy desk with space to work

My astronaut friend loves this page on study spaces...

Piles of books and folders make it hard to get to notes quickly — if you can, use a bookshelf to keep them tidy and accessible. Also avoid clutter and rubbish on your desk, as important things can get lost whenever everything is on top of each other.

6

Coping with Stress

Exam periods can be stressful and it's normal to feel some nerves when you have an exam approaching. Luckily there are ways to cope so stress doesn't affect your revision or your health.

Exams are Stressful for Everyone

1) You won't be alone in feeling under pressure about exams — it's likely your classmates are also finding this time stressful.

2) A small amount of stress can be good for you — it can motivate you to do better or help you focus on overcoming a difficult situation.

3) However, too much stress can negatively impact your health. It's important to recognise the signs of stress so you can do something about them.

Signs of Stress include:

- A loss of appetite
- Sudden weight loss or gain
- Feeling anxious
- Difficulty concentrating
- Feeling emotional
- Struggling to sleep

There Are Ways to Help With Stress...

1) Go outside for exercise and fresh air — it will help you clear your head.

2) Set aside time to meet up with your friends where you're not revising.

3) Give yourself relaxation time — listen to music, watch TV or doze outside in the sun.

4) Keep up with your hobbies and doing activities you enjoy.

5) Eating and sleeping well can also help with reducing stress (see p.7).

11.45am–12.45pm	12.45pm–1:30pm
Lunch - with Annie and Abed	Maths - Algebra

Talk about how you're feeling

Talking to friends, family and teachers can really help you air out your anxieties and come up with a way to deal with your stress. If you don't feel comfortable talking to people you know, there are support services and helplines who you can talk to confidentially.

... And Ways to Make it Worse

1) Don't revise late into the evening — this will affect your sleep and make you tired.

2) Not taking adequate breaks will make your revision time less effective (see p.48).

3) Don't set unrealistic targets or you'll always disappoint yourself.

Bottling up your stress is no laughing matter — tell people how you feel...

Exams are important, but they're not worth affecting your health. Make sure you take time out from revision to do things you enjoy — not only will this make you happier, it'll also make revising easier.

Sleep and Diet

Ah, my two favourite things in the world — snoozing and food. Getting a healthy amount of both these things will keep you at peak condition when you're revising and make it easier to take in information. Yum.

1) Don't Skip Sleep to Revise

Sleep helps you process what you've learnt.

2) Avoid Pricking Your Finger on a Spindle

Otherwise you'll sleep for a hundred years... wait, that's for a different book...

3) Do Something Relaxing Before Bed

Avoid caffeine, strenuous exercise and looking at your phone.

4) Sleep on Your Revision Notes

You'll revise through osmosis. If you don't know what osmosis is, sleep on a biology book tonight...

5) Keep Your Phone Away From Your Bed

It'll disrupt your sleep if it keeps going off.

6) Eat Plenty of Fruit and Veg

Yes, even broccoli (honestly, you grow to like it).

7) Don't Skip Meals

It makes it difficult to concentrate.

8) Get Plenty of Protein

Oily fish are great to eat (but hard to catch).

9) Only Have Sweets and Chocolate as an Occasional Treat

This was harder for me to write than it was for you to read.

10) Drink Lots of Water

From a glass, from a mug, from a bowl if you're a maverick.

The Perfect Cup of Tea

The making and drinking of tea are important life skills. It's not something that's likely to crop up in any of your exams, but it is something that will make your revision much easier. So here's a guide to making the perfect cuppa...

1) Choose the Right Mug

A good mug is an essential part of the tea drinking experience, but choosing the right vessel for your tea can be tricky. Here's a guide to choosing your mug:

Some <u>bad</u> mugs:

<u>No</u> handles.

Too <u>fancy</u> (and saucers are for grannies).

Too <u>flimsy</u> (and too <u>80s</u>).

<u>Too many</u> handles.

The <u>perfect</u> mug:

Holds just the <u>right amount</u> of tea.

Wide enough to <u>dunk a biscuit</u>.

Has a <u>design</u> that <u>complements</u> your <u>personality</u>.

Nice, <u>easy to hold</u> handle.

2) Get Some Water and Boil It

For a <u>really great brew</u> follow these easy step-by-step instructions:

1) First, pour some <u>water</u> into a <u>kettle</u> and switch it <u>on</u>. (Check it's switched on at the wall too.)
2) Let the kettle <u>boil</u>. While you're waiting, see what's on **TV** later and check your belly button for fluff. Oh, and put a <u>tea bag</u> in a <u>mug</u>.
3) Once the kettle has boiled, <u>pour</u> the water into the mug.
4) <u>Mash</u> the tea bag about a bit with a spoon. <u>Remove</u> the tea bag.
5) Add a splash of <u>milk</u>.

Note: some people may tell you to add the milk before the tea. Scientists have recently confirmed that this is nonsense.

3) Sit Back and Relax

Now this is important — once you've made your cuppa:

1) Have a quick rummage in the kitchen cupboards for a <u>cheeky biscuit</u>. (Custard creams are best — steer clear of any ginger biscuits — they're <u>evil</u>.)
2) Find your <u>favourite</u> armchair/beanbag. Move the cat.
3) Sit back and enjoy your mug of tea. You've <u>earned it</u>.

Phew — time for a brew I reckon...

It's best to ignore what other people say about making tea and follow this method. Trust me, this is the most definitive and effective method. If you don't do it this way, you'll have a shoddy drinking experience.

Learn, Revise, Test Yourself

This process is super important. You can't revise what you don't understand, or practise what you don't know, so don't skip out steps — there's no time for monkeying around.

LEARN

The learning process starts in school and with homework, but sometimes you might have to do some extra research too.

Before you start revising a topic, you need to make sure that you understand it.

If there's anything you're not sure about, you could:
- look back over your notes carefully and read the textbook again.
- do some research, in the library or online.
- ask your teacher.

REVISE

When you're happy that you understand a topic, you can move on to revise it.

Revising is the process of going back over what you've learnt so that you're ready to answer questions on it in an exam.

There are many different ways to revise — here are just a few examples:
- condensing your notes (see p.10-11)
- mind maps (see p.12-13)
- flow charts (see p.14-15)
- flashcards (see p.16-17)

Don't worry if you find something you don't understand — just go back and learn it again.

To make a topic stick, test yourself on it at increasing intervals after revising it, e.g. after half an hour, after two hours, after a day etc.

TEST YOURSELF

Once you're happy that you know a topic, it's time to test yourself:

- You could start by doing some quick fact recall questions, and then go on to some practice exam questions.

- It's really important to do some realistic exam practice — some questions will ask you to apply what you've learnt in different ways so it's good to know you can do this.

If there's something you can't remember, go back to your notes and revise it again.

Condensing Your Notes

Now you know how to get started, it's time to get cracking. The first step is to get your notes into order — you can't learn every word you've ever written so you need to condense them. Here we go...

Start With Your Notes

1) You'll need to start off with some <u>high-quality</u> notes, including:
   - A <u>CGP Revision Guide</u> (the perfect revision companion, of course)
   - your <u>class notes</u>
   - <u>text books</u>
   - <u>revision sheets</u> from your teacher

2) <u>Read over</u> them and make sure you <u>understand</u> what you've read — simplifying a topic into <u>key points</u> won't help you if you don't understand your original notes.

Condense Them In Your Own Words

1) You'll want to <u>simplify</u> and <u>summarise</u> your notes into <u>key points</u> so they're easier to revise from.

2) Aim to get <u>each topic</u> onto a <u>single page</u>. <u>Cut</u> out the <u>waffle</u> and pick out what's <u>important</u>.

3) Try to <u>reorganise</u> the material in some way, e.g. by <u>grouping</u> it differently or <u>linking</u> topics together.

4) How you present your notes might depend on the subject. For example, you could make:

<u>Labelled</u> <u>diagrams</u> for <u>Science</u>.

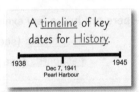

A <u>timeline</u> of key dates for <u>History</u>.

1938   Dec 7, 1941   1945
        Pearl Harbour

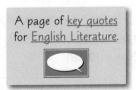

A page of <u>key quotes</u> for <u>English Literature</u>.

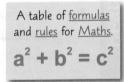

A table of <u>formulas</u> and <u>rules</u> for <u>Maths</u>.

$$a^2 + b^2 = c^2$$

5) Condensing topics makes your revision <u>interactive</u> — it's better than just re-reading your notes again. Plus, you're more likely to remember your <u>own words</u> than something someone else has written*.

Test Yourself On What You've Covered

When you've simplified a topic, it's time to <u>test yourself</u>:

1) <u>Cover up</u> your notes and <u>write down</u> as much as you can remember.

2) <u>Compare</u> what you've written to your notes then <u>fill in any gaps</u> — use a <u>different colour</u> so you know which bits you missed.

3) <u>Keep doing this</u> until you remember everything on the topic.

> It's a good idea to come back and test yourself again later, to see what you can still remember. (See more about spaced practice on p.50.)

---

*apart from my words — you'll definitely remember my words...

The key to condensing is to pick out the right points. If it helps, you might want to go through and highlight the important bits before you start writing. There's no 'right' way of doing it, just the way that works for you.

Condensing Your Notes

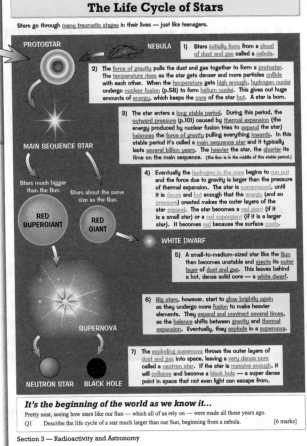

EXAMPLE:

Here is a page on The Life Cycle of Stars, from a CGP GCSE Physics Revision Guide.

Here is an <u>example</u> of how you could <u>condense</u> the info down into the <u>key points</u>:

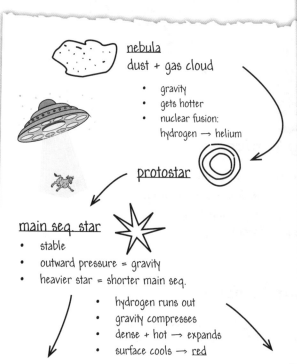

<u>nebula</u>

dust + gas cloud

- gravity
- gets hotter
- nuclear fusion:
  hydrogen → helium

<u>protostar</u>

<u>main seq. star</u>

- stable
- outward pressure = gravity
- heavier star = shorter main seq.

  - hydrogen runs out
  - gravity compresses
  - dense + hot → expands
  - surface cools → <u>red</u>

<u>red supergiant</u>

<u>red giant</u>

<u>white dwarf</u>

- smallish stars → unstable
- ejects outer layer
- hot, dense solid core left behind

<u>neutron star</u>

- after explosion
- very dense core

BANG!!

<u>supernova</u>

- big stars → more fusion
- creates heavy elements
- expand, contract, EXPLODE!

<u>black hole</u>

- biggest stars
- light can't escape

Revision Techniques

Drawing Mind Maps

If you say 'mind map' as fast as you can 40 times while looking at a topic, one will draw itself...

A Mind Map is a Type of Diagram

1) Mind maps are a <u>visual</u> way to <u>organise information</u>.

2) <u>One mind map</u> usually represents <u>one topic</u>.

3) The <u>name</u> of the topic goes in the <u>middle</u>, with <u>sub-topics</u> and further <u>detail</u> added around it.

4) Details are <u>short</u> and <u>to the point</u>.

5) <u>Boxes</u> or <u>bubbles</u> around some of the information can help it <u>stand out</u>.

6) A good mind map uses <u>colour</u> and <u>images</u>.

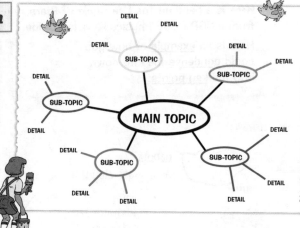

Mind Maps Are Great For Revising Topics

1) Organising material <u>visually</u> can make it <u>easier to recall</u> in an exam.

2) <u>Colour</u> and <u>images</u> can help topics and information to stick in your memory.

3) Mind maps can help you to identify the <u>key ideas</u> of a topic and find <u>links</u> between them, which can help you see the topic in different ways.

You Can Use Them Throughout Your Revision

Mind maps are really useful for <u>subjects</u> where there are <u>lots of links</u> between ideas (e.g. <u>History</u> or <u>English</u>) but less useful for learning a list of formula or a vocab list.

At the start

Use your notes and other resources to <u>draw a mind map</u> of a topic — it's a great way of <u>revising key information</u>.

During revision

You could <u>pin</u> your completed mind maps <u>up</u> in your revision space so that you <u>see them regularly</u>.

To test yourself

<u>Draw a mind map</u> of a topic from <u>memory</u>, then refer to the original and <u>fill in any gaps</u> in a <u>different colour</u> — this shows you what you <u>still need to revise</u>.

They told me to mind my own business...

... so I minded my business, my history, my maths, my geography. Making and using mind maps will make your revision really effective (and *deep breath* enjoyable...) so grab your compass and go exploring.

Drawing Mind Maps

EXAMPLE:

Here is an example of a mind map for the poem **'The Manhunt'** by <u>Simon Armitage</u>.
It <u>isn't complete</u>, but it gives you an <u>idea</u> of <u>where to start</u>.

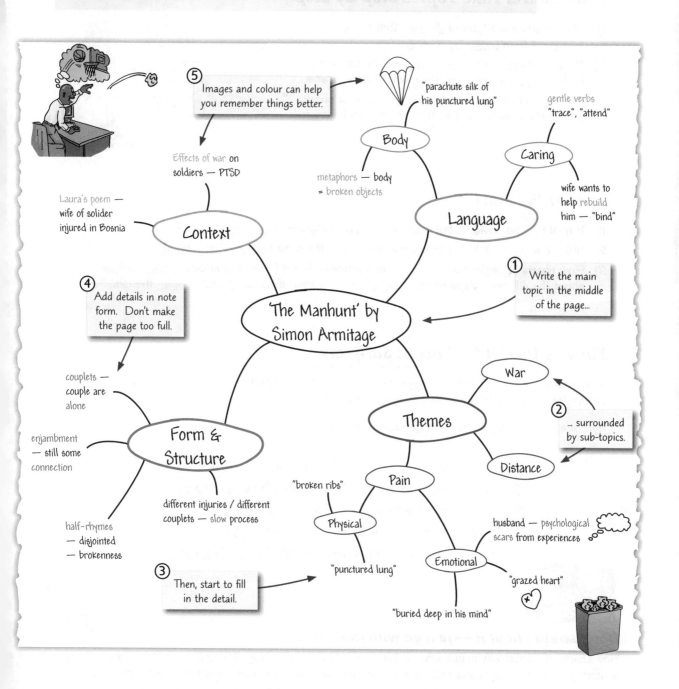

⑤ Images and colour can help you remember things better.

"parachute silk of his punctured lung"

gentle verbs "trace", "attend"

Effects of war on soldiers — PTSD

Body

metaphors — body = broken objects

Caring

wife wants to help rebuild him — "bind"

Laura's poem — wife of solider injured in Bosnia

Context

Language

① Write the main topic in the middle of the page...

④ Add details in note form. Don't make the page too full.

'The Manhunt' by Simon Armitage

couplets — couple are alone

War

enjambment — still some connection

Form & Structure

Themes

② ... surrounded by sub-topics.

half-rhymes — disjointed — brokenness

different injuries / different couplets — slow process

Distance

"broken ribs"

Pain

Physical

husband — psychological scars from experiences

③ Then, start to fill in the detail.

"punctured lung"

Emotional

"grazed heart"

"buried deep in his mind"

Making Flow Charts

Flow charts are the next big thing. The talk of the town. Everyone's mad about them, haven't you heard? Don't just take my word for it though, read on and see for yourself... (gotcha, they're all my words too.)

Flow Charts Take Topics Step By Step

1) Flow charts are a type of <u>diagram</u> that show a <u>process</u> from <u>beginning to end</u>.

2) They <u>organise information clearly</u> — you can use both <u>words</u> and <u>images</u> to show what happens when.

3) It's tempting to spend ages making your flow charts look perfect but as long as they're <u>clear</u> and <u>easy to use</u>, they don't need to be fancy.

Start at the Start

1) It might sound obvious, but <u>order</u> is really important in <u>flow charts</u>.

2) Write the <u>first step</u> in the process at the <u>top</u> of the page and <u>work downwards</u>.

3) Flow charts highlight the <u>main steps</u> in a process, but if it helps, you can <u>add key points</u> about the different steps to <u>jog your memory</u> — keep them <u>short</u> and <u>concise</u> though.

They're Useful for Lots of Subjects

Flow charts show how different <u>stages or events</u> are <u>linked</u> together, so they're useful for subjects that include <u>sequences</u> or <u>processes</u>.

Here are a few examples of when you might use them:

<u>Business Studies</u> — to show the different stages within a <u>supply chain</u>.

<u>History</u> — a <u>timeline</u> of the events that led to the <u>Great Depression</u>.

<u>Chemistry</u> — to set out the steps of a <u>practical experiment</u>.

<u>Geography</u> — to present the different stages of <u>erosion</u>.

<u>Biology</u> — to show how food passes through the <u>digestive system</u>.

Um, I think you missed a step...

Don't stress about it — just go with the flow...

Flow charts are a great way to mix your revision up and keep it engaging. Using the same techniques all the time is snoring (snore + boring, come on... keep up) and it's much harder to make information stick in your mind.

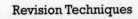

Making Flow Charts

This is an example of a flow chart you could make for Biology, showing how the <u>Central Nervous System responds to stimuli</u>. It doesn't show everything about the whole topic but it shows you how to get started.

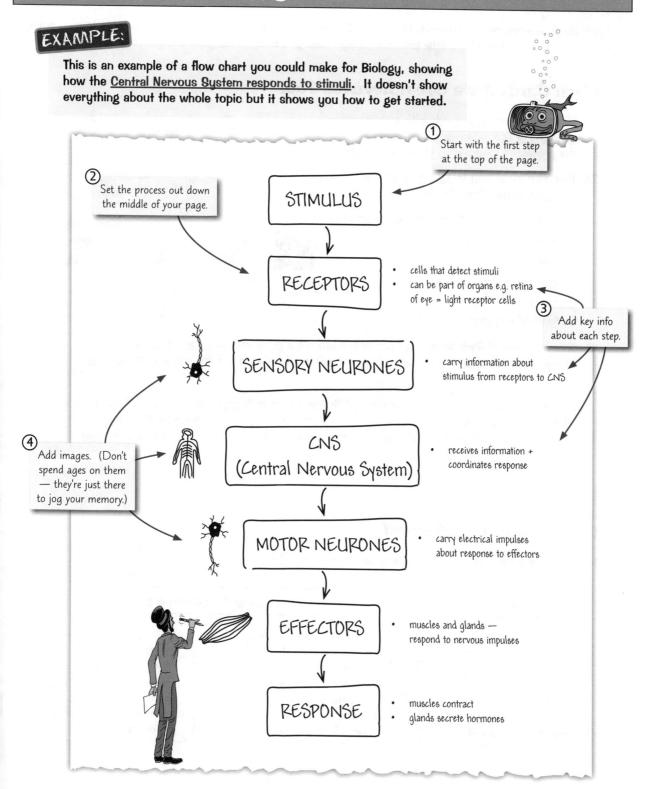

① Start with the first step at the top of the page.

② Set the process out down the middle of your page.

STIMULUS

RECEPTORS
- cells that detect stimuli
- can be part of organs e.g. retina of eye = light receptor cells

③ Add key info about each step.

SENSORY NEURONES
- carry information about stimulus from receptors to CNS

CNS (Central Nervous System)
- receives information + coordinates response

④ Add images. (Don't spend ages on them — they're just there to jog your memory.)

MOTOR NEURONES
- carry electrical impulses about response to effectors

EFFECTORS
- muscles and glands — respond to nervous impulses

RESPONSE
- muscles contract
- glands secrete hormones

Using Flash Cards

Flash cards are one of the simplest, but most effective, revision tools. You might not be able to play solitaire or snap with them, but with a little patience, they'll help you bridge any gaps and get to you to número uno.

Flash Cards Are a Great Revision Tool

1) Flash cards are small cards with a question or prompt on one side, and the answer or information on the other side.

2) They're a great way to test yourself and find gaps in your knowledge.

3) Flash cards are useful for learning things like:
   - important dates in History
   - language vocabulary
   - key words and definitions
   - formulae
   - labelled diagrams

   Flash cards aren't so good for learning things like processes and more complex information that can't be easily split up — take a look at the rest of this chapter for ideas on how to revise these.

4) There are lots of flash cards available online but it's a good idea to make your own. Working through your notes and picking out information is part of the process of revision.

Another great way to use flash cards is by filling one side with example questions about a topic, and the other side with the answers. This can be useful after you've revised a topic and want to test yourself on it. (I hear CGP do a pretty awesome range of revision question cards...)

Use Them to Test Yourself

Here are a few top tips on how to use your flash cards effectively:

Say your answers out loud — this forces you to answer the questions properly.

Test yourself until you get them all correct — make a pile of any cards you get wrong and go over them until you know them all.

Make sure you test yourself both ways — e.g. you need to know vocab translations from English to French and French to English.

Ask someone else to test you — it removes the temptation to check the other side yourself before answering.

Using Flash Cards

Flash Cards are *Easy to Make*

Anyone can make good flash cards (with not a magic trick in sight...) — here's how:

1) Write a <u>question or prompt</u> on <u>one side</u> of the card.

2) Add <u>colour</u> and any <u>quick pictures</u> that might help you recall the information.

3) <u>Complete the other side</u> with the <u>answer</u> or <u>piece of information</u>.

4) Keep your flash cards <u>simple</u> and stick to <u>one</u> piece of information <u>per card</u>.

5) And voilà! You have made a flash card appear and there's a rabbit somewhere out of a job...

EXAMPLE:

Here are a few examples of some flash cards you could make (front and back). They should be <u>clear</u> and <u>easy to read</u>:

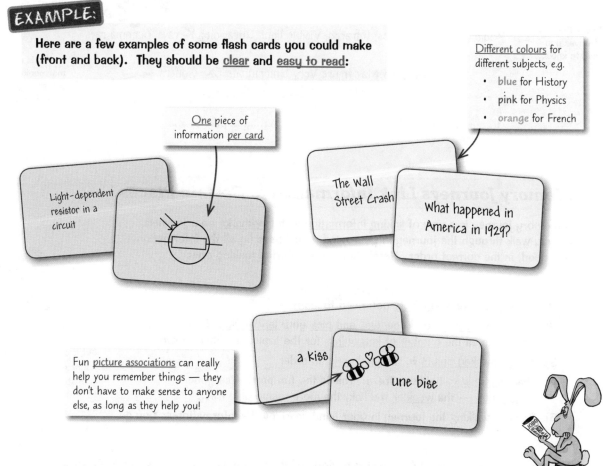

<u>One</u> piece of information <u>per card</u>.

Different colours for different subjects, e.g.
- blue for History
- pink for Physics
- orange for French

Light-dependent resistor in a circuit

The Wall Street Crash

What happened in America in 1929?

Fun <u>picture associations</u> can really help you remember things — they don't have to make sense to anyone else, as long as they help you!

a kiss

une bise

Flash cards — *lighting the way to revision success...*

Flash cards are so useful because they're pocket-sized — you can take them anywhere and test yourself on the go, really making the most of any time away from your desk without having to lug all your books around.

Memory Techniques

Trying to revise without memory techniques is a bit like an arrow with no end — totally pointless...

A Mnemonic is a Memory Device

1) A mnemonic is a way of remembering facts or information in a certain order.

2) The first letters of the words you need to know become the first letters of a sentence, song or rhyme — e.g. 'Richard Of York Gave Battle In Vain' to remember the colours of the rainbow.

3) A mnemonic can be anything, as long as it makes sense to you. However, funny or rude mnemonics tend to be easier to remember.

4) This example shows you a mnemonic to help you remember the electromagnetic spectrum in order of frequency:

This is the order of waves you need to know... → Radio waves, Microwaves, Infrared, Visible light, Ultraviolet, X-rays, Gamma rays

Raccoons May Injure Very Unfortunate EX-Golfers ← ... this is a mnemonic sentence you could learn.

Memory Journeys Link Information to Certain Places

A memory journey is a way of linking information with landmarks on a journey. As you walk through the journey in your mind, you'll pass by all the information you need, in the correct order. Here's how to get started making one:

1) Write down the key points you need to learn.

2) Choose a journey you know well and pick your landmarks. Pick as many landmarks as the number of key points for the topic. Jot them down.

3) Assign the key points to the landmarks in order.

4) Then, make links between them. This is the fun part! Use your imagination — the wackier the link, the more memorable it is.

5) Practise walking the journey in your mind, learning the information as you go.

It might take a while to get used to this technique but it can be really useful for recalling lots of information in exams.

Memory journeys are useful for learning all sorts of things, for example, processes in Science or sequences of events in History (there's an example of this on the next page...)

The Memory Journey

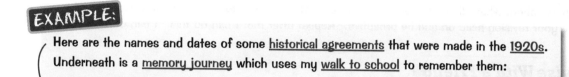

EXAMPLE:

Here are the names and dates of some <u>historical agreements</u> that were made in the <u>1920s</u>. Underneath is a <u>memory journey</u> which uses my <u>walk to school</u> to remember them:

1. Washington Conference 1921	4. Locarno Treaties 1925
2. Geneva Protocol 1924	5. Kellogg-Briand Pact 1928
3. Dawes Plan 1924	6. Young Plan 1929

The journey is there to jog your memory but you still need to learn the topics they're about in depth.

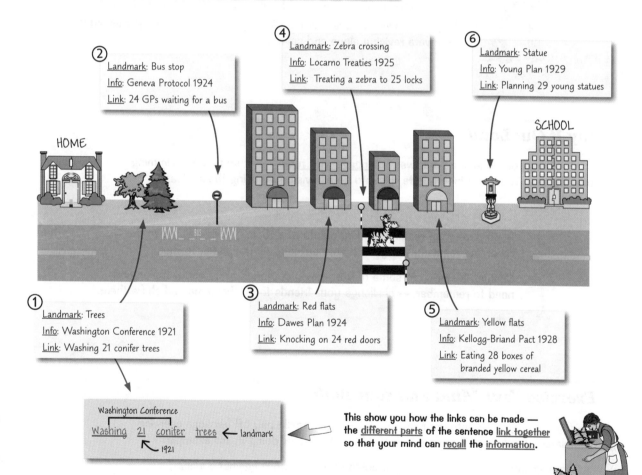

② **Landmark:** Bus stop
<u>Info</u>: Geneva Protocol 1924
<u>Link</u>: 24 GPs waiting for a bus

④ **Landmark:** Zebra crossing
<u>Info</u>: Locarno Treaties 1925
<u>Link</u>: Treating a zebra to 25 locks

⑥ **Landmark:** Statue
<u>Info</u>: Young Plan 1929
<u>Link</u>: Planning 29 young statues

HOME

SCHOOL

① **Landmark:** Trees
<u>Info</u>: Washington Conference 1921
<u>Link</u>: Washing 21 conifer trees

③ **Landmark:** Red flats
<u>Info</u>: Dawes Plan 1924
<u>Link</u>: Knocking on 24 red doors

⑤ **Landmark:** Yellow flats
<u>Info</u>: Kellogg-Briand Pact 1928
<u>Link</u>: Eating 28 boxes of branded yellow cereal

Washington Conference
<u>Washing</u> 21 <u>conifer</u> <u>trees</u> ← landmark
        ↳ 1921

This show you how the links can be made — the <u>different parts</u> of the sentence <u>link together</u> so that your mind can <u>recall</u> the <u>information</u>.

Now if only I could remember where I put my passport...

Plan each journey carefully and go over it until you don't make any mistakes. Keep it simple though or you might confuse yourself — washing 24 zebras because they ate boxes of yellow GPs won't get you any marks...

More Revision Tips

Don't panic about what other people are doing, do what works for you. Be a revision warrior not a worrier — face your revision head on and be proactive. Repeat after me: I can do this. I can do this...

Revise With a Friend

1) Test each other on different topics, e.g. using <u>flash cards</u>.

2) Try speaking for a minute on a topic, then get your friend to <u>ask you questions</u> on it.

3) Come up with <u>funny</u> pictures or stories to help you remember information. Get <u>creative</u>!

- Revising with a friend can be useful, but it's best not to do it all the time — it can be <u>distracting</u> and it's important to do your <u>own revision</u> too.

- <u>Don't chat</u> while you're revising. Take <u>regular breaks</u>, as you would if you were revising alone and save your chatting for then.

Say It Out Loud

Saying things out loud is a great way to <u>engage with topics</u> — it stops you skimming over details. You could incorporate this into your revision by using these ideas:

- <u>Record yourself</u> reading the key points of a topic and then <u>listen</u> to the recording <u>regularly</u>. Say the points <u>out loud</u> as you listen to them.

- <u>Change</u> the <u>lyrics</u> to some of your <u>favourite songs</u> to be about topics you need to remember — challenge your friends to do the same and share them.

Exercise Your Mind and Your Body

<u>Incorporating exercise</u> into your <u>revision routine</u> can really pay off because exercise stimulates your brain. There are lots of different ways of doing it, for example:

- To help with <u>language revision</u>, you could hit a <u>tennis ball</u> against a wall, reciting a <u>different part of the verb table</u> every time it <u>bounces</u>.

- <u>Play catch</u> with a friend and say a <u>fact</u> about a topic or the <u>next step in a sequence</u> when the ball comes to you.

Know What You'll be Tested On

No one knows the future — except me. If you learn what gets tested, you'll know just how to get marks.

Learn *These Three Rhymes to Prepare for What Exams Test*

CHECK the SPEC

1) Look at the exam board <u>specifications</u> and <u>past papers</u> for <u>all</u> of your exams.

2) Specifications tell you what you <u>need to know</u> and <u>how</u> you'll be <u>tested</u>.

3) Past papers show you the <u>types of questions</u> that could come up.

KNOW the AOs

1) <u>Assessment Objectives</u> are broad statements about what you <u>need to show</u> in your exams.

2) They differ for each GCSE, but include things like <u>subject knowledge</u> and <u>analytical ability</u>.

3) You should <u>find out</u> exactly which AOs are tested in each of <u>your exams</u>.

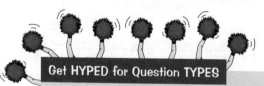

Get HYPED for Question TYPES

1) <u>Different question types</u> come up in <u>different exam papers</u> (e.g. you might get an extract in one English exam but not the other).

2) Make sure you know <u>which types of questions to expect</u>.

You can find specifications and Assessment Objectives on exam boards' websites. (Ask your teacher which ones you need.)

Find Out *What You'll Get Marks For*

It's important to know exactly <u>what to aim for</u> to earn those all-important marks. Here are a few ways to leave the examiner giddy with delight:

For <u>maths</u> questions, make sure you know when to <u>show your working</u>.

Use <u>specific vocabulary</u> and <u>examples</u> where possible (e.g. dates / locations in History.)

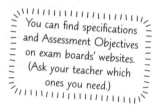

In science and maths, make sure <u>answers</u> are <u>realistic</u> and in the <u>correct units</u>.

<u>Check your writing</u> — some humanities exams give marks for SPaG.

Be prepared for questions about '<u>working scientifically</u>' in science exams.

My Geography teacher tried testing me on a volcano, but my pens melted...

I know, I know, you thought learning all your subject content was enough, and here I am telling you to learn about the exams too. Well, you've come this far, so take a breath and go check out some specs.

Make the Most of Practice Papers

While paper makes a rock-beating weapon, practice makes perfect — so it's important to get some done.

Do as Many Practice Questions as You Can

1) The key to successful revision is to ~~use a crystal ball~~ be <u>well prepared</u> for the exam. To do this, you need to know what exam-style questions look like.

2) Do as many <u>practice papers</u> as you can. CGP have plenty of practice papers — but they'll also be on exam board websites.

3) You can <u>warm up</u> by using your <u>notes</u> to help you, but it's also important to practise under <u>exam conditions</u>.

CGP's Practice Paper Top Tips

 ① <u>Practise under exam conditions</u>

- Get the <u>right equipment</u> out.
- <u>Time</u> yourself.
- Find somewhere quiet, with <u>no distractions</u>.
- <u>Don't use</u> your <u>revision notes</u> to help you.

② <u>Use the mark scheme</u>

- All practice papers should have <u>mark schemes</u>.
- These tell you how <u>marks are allocated</u> and how to get the <u>right answer</u>.*
- <u>Compare</u> the mark scheme to what you wrote.
- Mark yourself, <u>correcting</u> what you got wrong.

*Unfortunately, they don't tell you the meaning of life.

③ <u>Check out examiner's reports</u>

- These tell you what people struggled with, and the things <u>examiners look for</u> (besides love).
- Putting yourself in an examiner's shoes helps you see <u>how to improve</u> your answers.

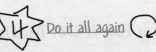 <u>Do it all again</u>

- Once you've marked your exam and figured out where you went wrong, <u>take a break</u> from it.
- After a day or two, <u>do the exam again</u>.
- This helps the <u>right answer</u> stick in your head.

⑤ <u>Don't panic</u>!!!!

- If you don't get a high mark at first, <u>don't worry</u> — the idea is to get <u>a bit better each time</u>.

Exam practice is just like washing your hair — you have to rinse and repeat...

... if you want to improve (/ have minty-fresh follicles). It's the same with jokes. I keep writing them so that one day I'll be funny. Your exams are no laughing matter though, so read the tips above and bust out a practice paper.

Command Words

Stop. Sit. Read. Follow these command words and you'll soon know all about the ones in your exams.

It's Important to Read the Question Carefully

 Read the question a <u>few times</u> (or until you <u>understand</u> it).

Use the <u>number of marks</u> available as a <u>guide</u> for <u>how long</u> to spend on a question.

 Hi, I'm Mark

Underline or circle <u>key</u> phrases and <u>command words</u>.

Command Words are Key — They Tell You What to Do

Common **Science** & **Maths** commands:

Command		Meaning
• Describe	→	talk through a process or trend
• Outline	→	state information about...
• Suggest	→	give possible causes for...
• Calculate	→	complete a calculation
• Show	→	prove something is true / false
• Explain	→	give reasons for something

Common **English** & **Humanities** commands:

Command		Meaning
• Discuss	→	talk about key points in detail
• How far do you agree?	→	give your opinion (and why)
• How important is...	→	discuss the significance of...
• How useful is...	→	weigh up the pros and cons of...
• Use evidence to show...	→	support a view with examples
• Explain	→	give reasons for something

 EXPLAIN YOURSELF!

EXAMPLE:

Here are some <u>example questions</u> that use command words.

Calculate the value of 'x'.

The command word here is '<u>calculate</u>', so you need to <u>work out a value</u>. E.g. "x = 5". Remember to show your working if the question asks you to.

Discuss the theme of creation in *Frankenstein*.

The command word here is '<u>discuss</u>', so you know this requires a <u>longer answer</u> that wants you to use <u>several different opinions</u> or bits of information.

Get to Know the Exams

Essay Skills

Right, it's time to look at the most useful skills in the world (apart from juggling of course). Here we go...

Take Some Time to Plan Your Answer

Planning helps you get your <u>ideas in order</u>, so you <u>don't run out</u> of <u>things to say</u> once you start writing.

For each essay question you get:
- **Read the <u>question</u> carefully.**
- **Read <u>every text</u> or source you need to.**
- **<u>Check</u> you know <u>how</u> to answer the question.**

Now <u>make a quick plan</u>:
- Jot down your main <u>ideas</u>.
- <u>Link</u> your ideas by topic or theme.
- <u>Outline</u> the <u>structure</u> of your answer.

And remember:
- **Don't spend <u>too long</u> planning.**
- **<u>Neatly cross out</u> your plan when you finish.**

SMASH IT

Write Well to Get Marks in Essay Questions

Structure Your Writing
- Use paragraphs to organise your points and link ideas.
- Link your paragraphs using phrases such as 'on the other hand' and 'in addition'.

You should aim to:
- Start with a <u>short introduction</u>.
- End with a brief summary / <u>conclusion</u> that <u>clearly reminds</u> the reader of your <u>main argument</u>.

Write Clearly
- Don't make your sentences too complicated.
- Check your argument is easy to understand.
- Use specific examples and precise quotes.

If you make a ~~misstacke~~ mistake, neatly cross it out and write the correction above.

Answer the question:
- Make sure you aren't just waffling.
- Make sure everything you write is relevant.
- Keep your ideas clear and to the point.

Essay Skills

Remember *That You are Writing For an Examiner*

Standard English

Make sure you <u>write properly</u>:

- <u>Avoid informal</u> words.
  (Romeo's <u>mate</u> Mercutio) ✗
- <u>Steer clear of slang</u>.
  (The poem made me <u>LOL</u>) ✗
- Don't use <u>filler words</u>.
  (Pollution is, <u>like</u>, bad) ✗

Standard English
helped Fleeflorb
fool his examiners...

Explaining Phrases

Explain things <u>clearly</u>
using phrases like:

- this signifies that...
- this highlights...
- this suggests that...
- furthermore...

These will keep your
answers <u>easy to follow</u>.

Linking Words

<u>Link</u> ideas and points
with words such as:

- however
- in contrast
- similarly
- alternatively

They will make your
answer <u>flow nicely</u>.

Don't Forget to Check *Your SPaG*

Some GCSE exams give you <u>marks</u> just for the <u>quality of your Spelling,
Punctuation and Grammar (SPaG)</u> — so it's well worth getting it <u>right</u>.

Recipe for Perfect SPaG:

1) Avoid <u>common spelling mistakes</u>
   (e.g. mixing up 'there' and 'their').

2) Use <u>punctuation properly</u> —
   remember to check it's all correct.

3) <u>Don't change tenses</u> by mistake —
   it's confusing and won't make sense.

4) Watch out for <u>double negatives</u> —
   avoid them in your essays.

5) Start a <u>new paragraph</u> for a <u>new point</u> —
   don't just write in one block of text.

6) Leave time to quickly <u>check your answers</u>.
   Take 5 minutes to fix any silly mistakes.

If you want to really master
<u>spelling, punctuation and grammar</u>,
take a peek at CGP's <u>SPaG range</u>.

All this talk of SPaG should help you pasta exams...

Writing clearly and having good SPaG is really important for essay questions. If you don't tick those boxes, then
you aren't making it as easy as possible for the examiner to understand your answers (and give you mega marks).

Weird Questions

Every so often, exams might hit you with something strange (like a fish). Don't fear though — help is here...

You Might Need to Tackle an Unusual Question in Your Exam

Oh no — you've flicked through your exam paper and seen a question that looks <u>totally unfamiliar</u>...

1. <u>Don't Panic</u> → 2. <u>Read it carefully</u> → 3. <u>Think it through</u> (It's probably just asking you to apply something you do know, but in a new way.)

EXAMPLE:

Sometimes Maths problems might be set in a real-life (wordy) <u>context</u>.
This means you have to work out <u>what you need to do</u> before you can do the maths:

> Elon buys apples in crates of <u>50 apples</u>. Each crate costs <u>£22.50</u>.
> He presses <u>3 crates</u> of apples <u>every weekday</u> (Mon-Fri) and <u>2 crates</u> per day at the <u>weekend</u>.
> How much will it cost Elon to buy enough crates of apples to keep pressing them for <u>5 weeks?</u>

Underlining the information you need can help.

Use what you've <u>underlined</u> to create the <u>correct calculations</u> for your answer:

Number of crates needed for 1 week = (3 x 5) + (2 x 2) = 19
Number of crates needed for 5 weeks = 19 x 5 = 95
Total cost of every crate needed = 95 x £22.50 = £2137.50

PressMaster 5000

Be Prepared for Tricky (But Predictable) Questions

If you know <u>certain types of questions</u> are <u>bound to come up</u>, you can <u>be ready</u> for them.

History: Using Sources

In History, you can get questions which ask you to decide how <u>useful</u> <u>a source</u> is — these can be <u>tricky</u>. It might help to ask yourself:

<u>Does any info make the source more / less reliable?</u>

Consider:
- <u>Who</u> wrote it
- Who they <u>wrote it for</u>
- <u>Why</u> they wrote it

<u>Does the source match what you know about the topic?</u>

- Compare <u>what you know</u> about the topic with the <u>information</u> in the source.
- If they <u>don't match</u>, think about <u>why</u>.

<u>Does the source tell the full story?</u>

- Consider whether the source leaves out <u>key information</u>.
- The source may be unreliable if the writer is <u>deliberately</u> trying to <u>hide something</u>.

Weird Questions

English Literature: Unseen Poetry

It can be tough not knowing which <u>poems</u> will come up. Whatever happens, remember to:

1) <u>READ</u> the poem — work out <u>what it's about</u>.
2) <u>IDENTIFY</u> the poem's message — think about <u>why</u> the poet wrote it.
3) <u>EXPLORE</u> emotions and feelings — consider the poem's <u>mood</u>.
4) <u>PICK OUT</u> literary techniques — explain their <u>effect</u> and use <u>quotes</u>.
5) <u>INCLUDE</u> your thoughts — think about how the poem <u>made you feel</u>.

Science: Calculation Questions

A good chunk of marks are available for <u>calculation questions</u>.
If you find <u>maths</u> daunting, these things can help:

Show Your Working Out ⟶ You get <u>marks</u> for it and it can help you <u>spot silly errors</u>.

Check Your Answer ⟶ Make sure your answer <u>seems sensible</u>.

Read Tables / Graphs Carefully ⟶ Double check you've used the <u>correct figures</u>.

Geography: Case Studies

Think of Case Studies as <u>detailed examples</u>. You'll be asked to <u>evaluate</u>, <u>explain</u> or <u>suggest</u> things based on your knowledge. When answering Case Study questions:

<u>Avoid general answers</u> that could be about anywhere.

Use <u>clear</u> and <u>specific details</u> (e.g. dates, place names, events).

<u>Answer the question</u> — don't just write out every fact you know.

EXAMPLE:

 There was an earthquake in Italy that caused lots of damage.

 In <u>2009</u>, over <u>300</u> people in L'Aquila (Italy) died following an earthquake which left more than <u>60,000</u> people homeless.

Do dogs have eyebrows, or do some eyebrows just have legs?

Don't let these pages panic you too much — it's unlikely you'll get asked anything really weird in your exam. It's still a good idea to be prepared for all the tricky things that might come up though, just in case...

Maths

Additional revision tips coming your way, divided into different subjects. You might wish you could subtract Maths from your life, but these handy tips will give you warm, fuzzy feelings for it that will only multiply.

Practice *is the Best Revision*

1) The best way to revise maths is by doing <u>practice questions</u>.
2) Start by practising questions on <u>specific topics</u> once you've revised them.
3) Then do <u>practice papers</u> to test a <u>mixture of topics</u> — this will help you <u>identify weak areas</u> (see p.22).

Remember *Formulas* with *Flash Cards*

1) Flash cards are good for learning <u>formulas</u>.
2) Write a <u>prompt</u> on one side of the card, and the <u>formula</u> on the other side (see <u>p.16-17</u> on how to use flash cards).
3) Some <u>formulas aren't given</u> in the exam so you need to learn those formulas as part of your revision.

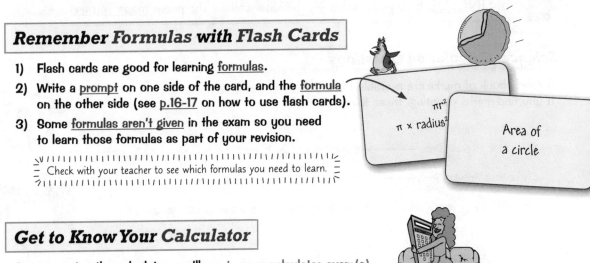

Check with your teacher to see which formulas you need to learn.

πr^2

$\pi \times radius^2$

Area of
a circle

Get to *Know* Your Calculator

<u>Practise</u> using the calculator you'll <u>use in your calculator exam(s)</u>.

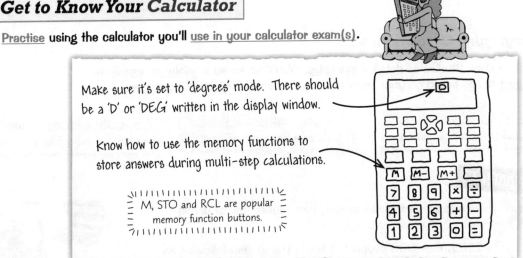

Make sure it's set to 'degrees' mode. There should be a 'D' or 'DEG' written in the display window.

Know how to use the memory functions to store answers during multi-step calculations.

M, STO and RCL are popular memory function buttons.

Use memory functions to avoid rounding too early

If you get an answer with lots of <u>decimal places</u> during a multi-step question, use the <u>memory function</u>. You can then <u>use that number</u> for the next step instead of rounding, which may affect your final answer.

Maths

Understand *What a Question is Asking*

1) Know what each <u>command word</u> wants you to do.
2) Use the <u>number of marks</u> as a guide to <u>how much time</u> you should spend on a question.
3) Show your <u>working out</u> — marks are given for it.
4) Answer in the <u>correct units</u>, or to the correct number of <u>significant figures</u> or <u>decimal places</u>.

Command Words

- <u>Write down</u>/<u>state</u> — give a brief answer
- <u>Calculate</u>/<u>find</u>/<u>solve</u> — show your working out
- <u>Explain</u> — give a written reason for your answer

EXAMPLE:

Take a look at this exam question. There are plenty of ways to avoid losing easy marks.

---

11 The formula for the period, *T* seconds, of a pendulum of length *l* metres is given by:

$$T = 2\pi\sqrt{\frac{l}{g}}$$

At the equator, *g* = 9.78 m/s².

(a) Find the period of a pendulum, of length 30 cm, at the Equator. Give your answer to 3 significant figures.

T = ... seconds
[2]

You're given a length in centimetres, but the formula uses lengths in metres. You need to convert 30 cm into metres.

The command word is 'find' so you need to show your working out.

Make sure you round your final answer to 3 significant figures.

You need to answer the question in seconds.

Check *Your Answer Makes Sense*

1) Make sure your answer is <u>sensible</u> — a person can't be 22 m tall.
2) Check for <u>silly mistakes</u> — 3 × 3 is not 6.
3) If you've solved an equation, put the <u>answer</u> back <u>into the equation</u> to see if it's correct.
4) <u>Expand factorised brackets</u> to check they give you the original expression.

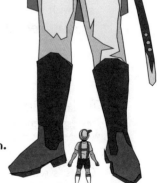

I always check every page I write for chicken silly mistakes...

One of the (many) great things about GCSE Maths is that most questions have definite answers, meaning you can check whether you've got the right answer. Maths gets a bad rap sometimes, but it's actually very generous.

Science

You and revision probably have quite the chemistry now, so you'll be glad to hear there are things you can do together to help with your science exams. Not that you two need an excuse to spend time with each other...

Match Pairs to Learn Key Terms

1) Write <u>key terms</u> and their <u>definitions</u> on separate pairs of cards. Then jumble and <u>sort the pairs</u>.

2) When you can sort them all, try <u>recalling the definitions</u> based on the <u>term only</u>.

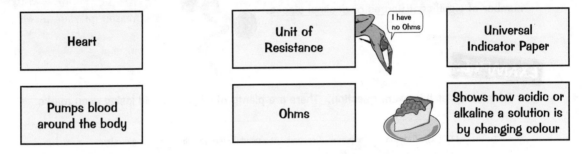

Heart	Unit of Resistance	Universal Indicator Paper
Pumps blood around the body	Ohms	Shows how acidic or alkaline a solution is by changing colour

I have no Ohms

Remember Scientific Processes With Storyboarding

To help you <u>remember processes</u> with many steps, you could <u>create stories</u>.

EXAMPLE:

You could storyboard the digestive system like this:

You can't describe processes in an informal way like this in the exam — you need to use scientific language and terminology.

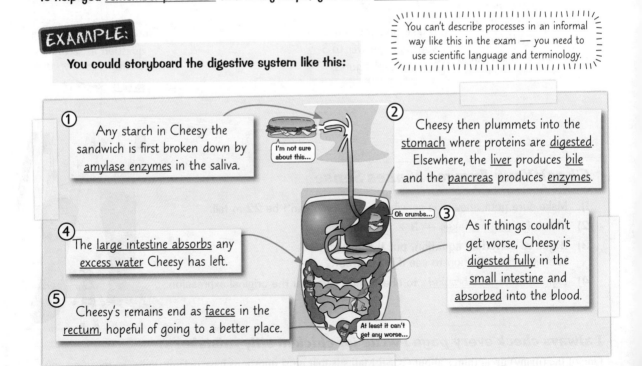

① Any starch in Cheesy the sandwich is first broken down by <u>amylase enzymes</u> in the saliva.

I'm not sure about this...

② Cheesy then plummets into the <u>stomach</u> where proteins are <u>digested</u>. Elsewhere, the <u>liver</u> produces <u>bile</u> and the <u>pancreas</u> produces <u>enzymes</u>.

Oh crumbs... ③ As if things couldn't get worse, Cheesy is <u>digested fully</u> in the <u>small intestine</u> and <u>absorbed</u> into the blood.

④ The <u>large intestine absorbs</u> any <u>excess water</u> Cheesy has left.

⑤ Cheesy's remains end as <u>faeces</u> in the <u>rectum</u>, hopeful of going to a better place.

At least it can't get any worse...

Science

Get to Grips with Practical Skills

Set aside time specifically for revising <u>practical-related skills</u>:

1) Learn the <u>names of equipment</u> and how to <u>improve the quality</u> of the data obtained.
2) Be familiar with how to <u>record data</u> — e.g. don't include units in the main body of a table.
3) Practise <u>drawing graphs</u>, using a ruler and sharp pencil for accuracy.

EXAMPLE:

Take a look at this practical skills exam question.

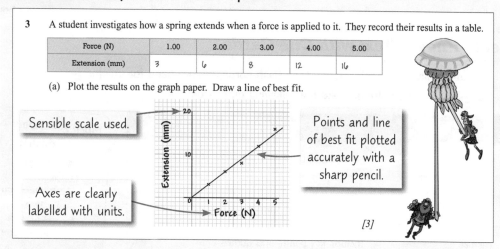

3   A student investigates how a spring extends when a force is applied to it. They record their results in a table.

Force (N)	1.00	2.00	3.00	4.00	5.00
Extension (mm)	3	6	8	12	16

(a) Plot the results on the graph paper. Draw a line of best fit.

Sensible scale used.

Points and line of best fit plotted accurately with a sharp pencil.

Axes are clearly labelled with units.

[3]

Know Which Formulas You Need to Learn

1) You're only given <u>some formulas</u> in the exam — you need to <u>learn</u> the ones that <u>aren't given</u>.
2) Practise using <u>every formula</u> so you can <u>use them all</u> confidently in the exam.

Get Key Vocabulary into Your Answers

1) Marks are awarded for using <u>correct terminology</u>.
2) Make sure you <u>learn key words</u> and their <u>meaning</u> as part of your revision.
3) In the <u>exam</u>, check that you've used <u>relevant scientific terms</u> correctly.

I don't trust atoms — I hear they make everything up...

But you won't when you've revised properly — here's a pretty useful formula to start you off: $GO_2D\ PL4N_2ING$.

English Literature

Fun fact — pneumonoultramicroscopicsilicovolcanoconiosis is the longest word you'll find in a dictionary. Fortunately, revising for your English Literature exam isn't nearly as daunting as trying to write that word.

Organise Your Revision for Each Text

1) Make a <u>separate folder</u> for each text you're studying throughout your GCSE.
2) When you finish reading a text, write a <u>short summary</u> of what it is about.
3) For longer texts, note down important <u>plot points</u> or <u>passages</u> too.
4) You can then <u>look back</u> at these notes when you <u>start revising</u>.

PNEUMONOULTRAMICROSCOPIC...ETC.

Close enough...

Get to Know a Text with Cue Cards

1) Cue cards have <u>more information</u> than flash cards and are used for <u>quick reference</u>.
2) For <u>every text</u> you study, make the following cue cards:

Card	Details
List of Characters	Names and brief description of who's who.
Main Characters	List each main character's characteristics and a quote that sums them up.
Themes	Include key points and quotes.
Context and Audience	When and why the text was written, and how the context affects the text.
Writer's language	Language techniques used by the writer and quotes that show these being used.

Much Ado About Nothing
Beatrice:
- Witty/Intelligent
- Outspoken
- Confident
- Loyal to Hero
- Annoyed by gender stereotypes
- Reluctant to marry

"she mocks all her wooers out of suit"

Make sure you only answer questions on the texts you've studied.

A Christmas Carol
Theme — Family:
- Happiness — Belle's family full of "joy, and gratitude".
- Loneliness — Scrooge was "a solitary child".
- Scrooge's change — becomes a "second father" to Tiny Tim.

3) You can use cue cards to revise a text in <u>different ways</u>:
- Read a set of cards for a <u>different text</u> frequently, e.g. <u>each day</u>.
- Put the cards somewhere <u>you'll see</u> them, e.g. on the fridge.
- Get a <u>friend</u> or <u>family member</u> to <u>test you</u> using your cards.

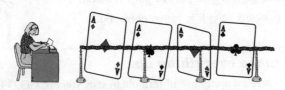

English Language

Language is a super word — there aren't many words that end in 'uage'. Jejune is also a great word — it means uninteresting, but this page isn't jejune. It's anti-jejune, jejuneless, jejune-free. I could go on...*

Read (and do) Practice Papers

1) Get used to the <u>type of questions</u> you'll be asked.

2) Practise <u>planning</u> and writing <u>answers out in full</u>.

3) The exam involves <u>analysing unseen texts</u>. Make sure you:

- <u>READ</u> the text carefully.
- <u>UNDERLINE</u> key words as you read the text.
- <u>NOTE</u> the writer's view after reading the text.

4) You'll need to <u>show the following skills</u> when answering questions:

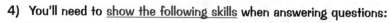

- Write <u>critically</u> and <u>clearly</u>
- "Use <u>quotes</u> to back up your points"
- Analyse <u>language</u>, <u>form</u> and <u>structure</u>
- Show you understand how <u>context</u> affects the text

5) You can find <u>past papers</u> for your exam board <u>online</u> (CGP do some practice papers too. Just sayin'...)

Creative Writing will Help for the Exam

1) You need to practise writing both <u>fiction</u> and <u>non-fiction</u> texts.

2) You also need to practise writing for <u>different audiences</u> and <u>purposes</u>. For example:

Write an article for a <u>broadsheet newspaper</u> in which you <u>explain</u> your point of view.

Write a speech for a debate at your <u>school</u> in which you <u>argue</u> for or against a statement.

3) To get top marks, your writing needs to be <u>interesting</u>, <u>accurate</u> and <u>well organised</u>.

4) Get <u>someone to read</u> your writing so you can get <u>feedback</u>.

Look at past papers for writing prompts to get your creative juices bubbling.

This page is jemarch, jeapril, jemay, but absolutely not jejune...

Be aware that English Literature and Language exams have different question types. You don't want to spend weeks practising writing *A Christmas Carol* fan fiction when you won't get asked to write one in either exam.

History

My teacher told me everything in GCSE History was in the past, so imagine my surprise when I found out that the exam was actually in the future. I got by though, and you can too with these handy tips.

Use Timelines to Revise Events

1) When answering questions, you need to be able to say <u>when events happened</u>.
2) Make a <u>timeline</u> to help you learn the <u>order</u> of <u>events</u>, e.g. for battles or new laws.
3) <u>Draw pictures</u> on your timeline as a way to <u>remember key events</u>.

EXAMPLE:

This is a timeline of the events leading to Hitler becoming Führer.

Learn <u>what happened</u> in each event too.

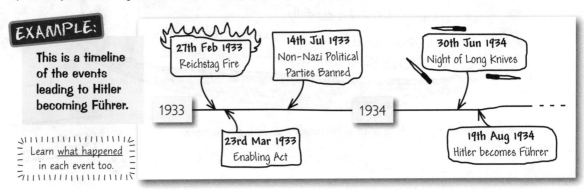

27th Feb 1933 Reichstag Fire

14th Jul 1933 Non-Nazi Political Parties Banned

30th Jun 1934 Night of Long Knives

1933   1934

23rd Mar 1933 Enabling Act

19th Aug 1934 Hitler becomes Führer

Revise the Causes and Consequences of Events

It's not enough to know <u>what happened</u> for each topic — you need to know <u>why the event happened</u> (the causes) and <u>what happened after the event</u> (the consequences).

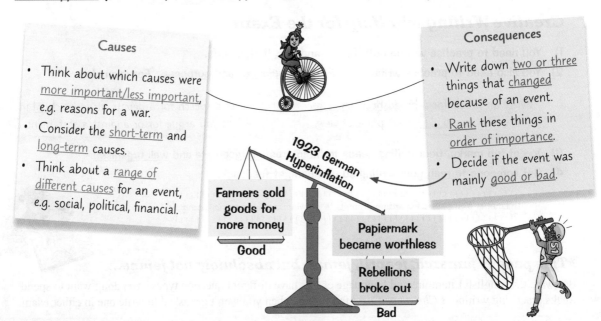

Causes

- Think about which causes were <u>more important/less important</u>, e.g. reasons for a war.
- Consider the <u>short-term</u> and <u>long-term</u> causes.
- Think about a <u>range of different causes</u> for an event, e.g. social, political, financial.

Consequences

- Write down <u>two or three</u> things that <u>changed</u> because of an event.
- <u>Rank</u> these things in <u>order of importance</u>.
- Decide if the event was mainly <u>good or bad</u>.

1923 German Hyperinflation

Farmers sold goods for more money
Good

Papiermark became worthless

Rebellions broke out
Bad

History

Tailor Your Answer to the Question

1) In the exam, double check the topic and dates mentioned in each question.
2) If the question asks about a date range, focus your answer on those years.
3) Be sure to answer the question — don't just write everything you know about a topic.
4) Back up each point you make with facts and details. For example:

> Life was hard for African Americans in 1920s America
> because segregation was widespread and many could not vote.

The only answer Hank won't tailor is fashion from last year...

Know the Different Question Types

1) Some questions in the exam require longer answers than others.
2) Questions worth a few marks only need a short answer.
3) Spend most of your time on essay questions which are worth more marks.

In the exam, make sure you answer the right number of questions — and on the right topics.

Short Questions

• Don't plan shorter answers — it wastes time.

• Don't spend loads of time on these questions.

• Learn the level of detail you need to pick up full marks.

Long Essay Questions

• Write a quick plan before you write your long answers.

• Talk about both sides of an argument.

• In your conclusion, say which side of the argument is strongest and why.

Knowing the usefulness of a source is another important skill — see page 26 for how to do this.

Double agents are like History essays — they talk about both sides...

Unlike spies though, your long essay answers shouldn't be subtle about mentioning both sides. Remember to include facts to back up any points you make and keep your answer focussed on the topic and time period stated.

Geography

You're in for a <u>world of fun</u> now — these pages will help <u>'Geog' your memory</u> before you tackle the exams.

Make Sure Your Map Skills are Strong

1) It's likely that <u>Ordnance Survey</u>® <u>maps</u> will appear in an exam. You need to know how to use <u>eastings</u> and <u>northings</u> to reference squares on a map grid:

- <u>Eastings</u> increase as you move east.
- <u>Northings</u> increase as you move north.
- Always write the <u>eastings value first</u>.

2) You also need to be able to work out the <u>distance between two places</u> on a map:

- Use a <u>ruler</u> to measure the distance between the places in <u>centimetres</u>.
- Compare your measurement to <u>the scale</u> to get the distance in <u>kilometres</u>.

EXAMPLE:

Give the <u>four figure reference</u> of the smiley face.

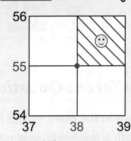

Four figure grid references give you a square.

- Find the <u>eastings</u> value for the left edge of the square the smiley is in — <u>38</u>.
- Find the <u>northings</u> value for the bottom edge of the square — <u>55</u>.
- So the reference is <u>3855</u>.

You'll Need to be Able to Discuss Photos and Graphs

Picking Apart Pictures

When <u>describing</u> a photo like the one on the right, go into <u>detail</u>:

- <u>Name features</u> (e.g. beaches, cliffs and arches).
- Describe <u>specific features</u> (e.g. how they were formed).

You might even be asked to describe <u>processes</u> that could be taking place in the photo (e.g. weathering or coastal erosion).

EXAMPLE:

Figure 1, a photo showing part of the Dorset coast in the UK.

Grappling with Graphs

- When <u>describing</u> graphs, always <u>refer to data</u> from the graph.
- Remember — a <u>line of best fit</u> shows a <u>trend</u>.
- Know that <u>scatter graphs</u> can show <u>+ve</u> or <u>-ve</u> <u>correlation</u>.

Geography

Be Prepared for Higher Mark Questions

Some questions in your Geography exam ask you to write a bit more (for a few more marks).

Use ADELE to remind you about what to include in your longer answers:

A — Accurate knowledge (facts and figures)

D — Detailed Understanding (make it clear that you 'get it')

E — Examples (include specific, relevant examples)

L — Links (use conjunctions, e.g. however, additionally, although...)

E — Evaluations (give your opinion or judgement)

Some longer answers will ask you to talk about Case Studies — see page 27 for how to manage these.

Don't Forget to Use the Right Terminology

1) Make sure you use the correct terminology and technical terms for processes.

2) It's important that you understand what key terms mean so that you can use them correctly in the exam.

Be Familiar with Maths

1) Some questions might ask you to use maths, so you need to know how to figure out:

- MODE = MOST common
- MEDIAN = MIDDLE value (when values are in order of size)
- MEAN = TOTAL of items ÷ NUMBER of items
- RANGE = DIFFERENCE between highest and lowest

2) You also need to be able to calculate percentages and percentage change:

- PERCENTAGE = (Part of Sample ÷ Total Sample) × 100

- PERCENTAGE CHANGE = $\dfrac{\text{Final value - original value}}{\text{original value}} \times 100$

Maths loved by all

What is central to understanding Geography? The letter 'r'...

Geography tests you on a wide range of skills, so you'll have to become familiar with all sorts in order to do your best in your exams. It's not all bad though — chances are you'll get plenty of nice pictures to look at...

Languages

Revising for a language exam can feel like... well... learning a foreign language. But don't worry, there's lots of tips on these pages to have you gabbling away like a native speaker.

Get To Know Your Vocab

Learning the vocab is really important, but you don't need to spend hours staring at vocabulary lists:

Turn your house into a dictionary
- Label items in your home such as rooms or furniture.

Make flashcards
- Write the vocab on one side of the card and the English word or a picture on the other side.
- Ask friends or family to test you.

Use your voice
- Say the vocab out loud to yourself or a friend.
- You could record yourself and then play it back.

Use Verb Tables to Learn Different Tenses

Verb tables are a great way to easily see the verb endings for different tenses.

Subject	Past	Present	Future
I			
You (sing)			
He/She/It			
We			
You (pl)			
They			

Make a table for each type of verb ending — pick a regular verb for each ending to use as an example.

Create blank copies of your table and test yourself by filling them out from memory — you could practise using different verbs.

Focus on Specific Verbs

1) Make a note of verbs you struggle to remember or often get wrong — irregular verbs tend to be the trickiest.

2) Make a verb table for each irregular verb. Use a different colour for the conjugations you find difficult, e.g. the verb 'dar' in Spanish:

3) Practise writing sentences using these verbs in different tenses — check the conjugations using your verb tables.

Subject	Present
I	doy
You (sing)	das
He/She/It	da
We	damos
You (pl)	dais
They	dan

Languages

Have The Examiner in the PALM of Your Hand

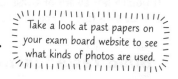

Take a look at past papers on your exam board website to see what kinds of photos are used.

In the <u>speaking exam</u>, you'll be given a <u>photo</u> to describe, with questions. You can practise for the speaking exam by <u>describing pictures</u>:

1) Use the <u>PALM</u> acronym to <u>note down vocabulary</u> to describe what is happening in the picture.

2) Use this vocabulary to <u>describe</u> the picture to a <u>friend or family member</u> — this step is important as you'll have to <u>say it out loud</u> in the speaking exam.

P = People
Who is in the picture?

A = Activity
What are they doing?

L = Location
Where are they?

M = Mood
How are they feeling?

Practise Useful Phrases

It's important to learn topic vocab, but there are more <u>general words and phrases</u> that will help you in the exams too. Spend some time <u>making</u> and learning <u>lists</u> of <u>different expressions</u> that will allow you to pick up <u>easy marks</u>:

(Opinion words:)   e.g. 'I think...', 'I believe...', 'Personally...'.

(Time expressions:)   e.g. 'tomorrow', 'last year', 'next weekend'.

(Conjunctions:)   e.g. 'therefore', 'but', 'because', 'consequently'.

(Comparisons:)   e.g. 'more than', 'less than', 'the same as', 'on the other hand', 'in contrast'.

I used the past, present and future in my language exam — it was intense...

Nothing else needs to be though — "bye bye tense, hello calm" (also PALM, don't forget PALM...). Don't panic if there's a word or phrase you don't recognise straight away — just see if you can use the context to work it out.

Chocolate Studies

If you're not aware of GCSE Chocolate Studies, you'll probably think this page is nonsense. However, if you are revising this completely real and totally not made-up subject, sink your teeth into some sweet knowledge.

Blind Taste Test to Learn Chocolate Types

1) In the exam, you'll need to know about <u>different types</u> of chocolate.
2) With a friend, get pieces of the main chocolate types — <u>dark</u>, <u>milk</u> and <u>white</u>.
3) Have your friend <u>blindfold you</u> and then pass you a <u>piece of chocolate</u>.
4) <u>Guess</u> the chocolate — your friend can tell you if you got it <u>correct</u>.

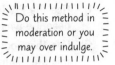

Do this method in moderation or you may over indulge.

Don't show preference to one type of chocolate

<u>Examiners</u> will have their favourite type of chocolate, so you need to discuss them <u>all equally</u> in any <u>exam-style question</u>.

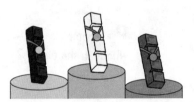

Know Important Chocolate Quotes

Use flashcards (p.16-17) to help you memorise these and other important quotes.

Chuck Alot, Chocolate Philosopher — 'Better to have had chocolate and lost, than to have never had chocolate at all.'

Botanist, Dame Cara Mel — 'A people without the knowledge of chocolate is like a tree without roots.'

Life Guru, Candice Cane — 'The journey of a thousand chocolates begins with one bite.'

Learn These Uses for Chocolate

Good Uses

Coins

Buttons

Fingers

You'll need to explain why chocolate is good and bad in different forms.

Bad Uses

Teapot

Dress (especially in summer...)

Tastes good though...

Hammer and Nails

Religious Studies

You're unlikely to be asked to write an answer evaluating the ethical statement 'It's always good to revise', but it's something I'm sure we can agree on. Continue your path to revision enlightenment with this page.

Learn Beliefs *and* Practices *in Detail*

When revising religious beliefs and practices, get used to doing these <u>three things</u>:

① Explain what the <u>belief means</u>.

② Link the belief to a <u>teaching or quote</u>.

③ Explain why the belief is significant to <u>religious people today</u>.

EXAMPLE:

Here's how you might revise a religious belief:

Belief ⟶ Christians believe humans are made in God's image.

What it means ⟶ Christians believe that God made all humans like Him, so everyone is important.

Quote / Teaching ⟶ In Genesis 1:26, God said "Let us make mankind in our image".

Significance Today ⟶ Christians may support charities which tackle injustice or inequality, because they believe that every person is valuable and should be treated with respect.

Debate *Ethical Questions*

1) With a friend or family member, decide on an <u>ethical statement,</u> e.g. 'The death penalty is always wrong'.

2) <u>Toss a coin</u> to decide who is in favour and who is against the statement.

3) Take <u>two minutes each</u> to put forward <u>established arguments</u> for or against it.

4) Turn it into a <u>game</u> — <u>give points</u> for examples, religious teachings and key terms.

Your suit is amazing.

I can't argue with that.

Learn to *Tackle Essay Questions*

1) Make sure all of your essay answers give <u>balanced viewpoints</u> and <u>refer to religion</u>.

2) Remember that there are often <u>differences of opinion within a religion</u>, e.g. Protestants and Catholics hold different viewpoints on different topics.

3) Use <u>precise examples</u>, e.g. 'An example of natural evil is natural disasters, <u>such as hurricane Katrina.</u>'

4) Essays should always have a <u>conclusion</u>, where you can give your <u>opinion</u> on what you've discussed.

I've tried provoking fish into arguments — they never take debate...

You'll end up revising a lot of serious ethical topics — try debating something light-hearted for a laugh, like 'cows are the best farm animal to take ice fishing' (I'd hate to argue against that one...).

Business Studies

I had this great idea to open hundreds of coffee shops which sold fancy-named drinks to people who liked being on their laptop in public. I couldn't get a financial backer though — something about competitors...

Learn Key Business Definitions

1) Learn business definitions, particularly for the multiple-choice questions.

2) Longer questions may also give a mark for knowledge of key terms.

3) The best way to learn these definitions is using flash cards (see p.16-17).

Make sure you're familiar with the different command words that come up so you know what you're being asked to do.

Read Case Studies Carefully

1) For questions that are based on case study information or on data, make sure you use evidence from the case study or data set as well as your knowledge of Business in your answer.

2) Before you get started, read the case study and any data all the way through. Then read the whole question carefully and make sure you've understood what you're being asked to do.

3) If you're asked to evaluate something, make sure you produce a balanced argument that discusses the positives and negatives, even if you then come to a conclusion supporting one side.

THIS JUST IN

YOU SHOULD TAKE AN INTEREST IN BUSINESS NEWS

- CASE STUDIES ARE BASED ON REAL BUSINESS CHALLENGES

- WATCHING BUSINESS NEWS WILL MAKE YOU AWARE OF KEY ISSUES

- YOU'LL LEARN REAL-LIFE EXAMPLES

Practise Your Maths Skills

1) Maths crops up a fair bit — you need to be able to do the following:

- Use maths in a business context, e.g. calculating the average rate of return.
- Interpret data and draw graphs, e.g. reading or plotting a total revenue line.
- Use formulas, e.g. to calculate the break-even point.

2) In an exam, show your workings and any formulas used — this may get you marks.

3) Make sure you give your answer to the number of decimal places that the question asks for.

Before the Exam

It's what this whole book has been preparing you for — the big exam day. However, to make sure you're in tip-top exam-slamming condition, here are some last-minute things you can do.

Do Final Preparations the Night Before

Spend time the night before the exam making sure you're prepared:

1) Eat a balanced meal (see p.7).
2) Get anything you're taking into the exam ready to go.
3) Double check where and when your exam is.
4) Do something relaxing or some gentle exercise.
5) You could read over some notes, but don't cram all night.
6) Try to get a good night's sleep (see p.7).

Exam Kit Checklist

- Multiple pens and pencils ☑
- A rubber and sharpener ☐
- A clear pencil case ☑
- A clear water bottle with no labels ☐
- Subject-specific stationery, ☐ e.g. ruler, calculator etc.

Wake Up at a Sensible Time

Set an alarm to make sure you wake up.

1) Give yourself time to wake up and get ready for your exam.
2) Eat a healthy breakfast with a glass of water and fruit.
3) If you have time, look over your notes at any key definitions, formulas, facts and quotes.
4) Don't revise anything new — save your energy for the exam.

Arrive at Your Exam in Plenty of Time

1) Leave home with more time than you need to get to your exam.
2) But try not to arrive too early — you don't want a long, nervous wait.

Waiting with other people

If people outside the exam hall seem stressed when you arrive, try to stay calm and not let their worries affect you. It's okay to ask to be left alone if that's what you need to mentally prepare yourself.

I brought pens to my exam — I couldn't take the sheep and pigs in though...

If you struggle to get a good night's sleep or eat a big breakfast because you're nervous, don't panic — it's not the end of the world. You can still perform well in your exam as long as you keep calm and stay focused.

During the Exam

Whenever I entered an exam hall and took my seat, I always imagined an orchestra playing an epic soundtrack as if it was the climax of an action movie. I also did other, more helpful things too...

Organise *Your Desk Space*

While you're waiting for the exam to start:

1) Get your <u>pens</u> and <u>stationery</u> out.
2) Place your <u>water bottle</u> and <u>watch</u> on your desk.
3) Take some <u>deep breaths</u> to calm yourself.
4) <u>Fill in the front</u> of your exam paper.
5) <u>Listen to instructions</u> given by the invigilators.

Focus *on What You're Doing* During the Exam

1) <u>Read</u> each question <u>carefully</u>.
2) <u>Read</u> each question <u>carefully</u> — seriously, you might <u>miss something</u> if you <u>rush</u>.
3) <u>Answer every question</u> that you need to — and don't answer any that you don't.
4) If you're <u>not sure</u> of an answer, make an <u>educated guess</u>.
5) Keep an eye on the <u>time</u> so you stay <u>on track</u> (with time to <u>check your answers</u>).
6) Judge <u>how long</u> to spend on a question based on how many <u>marks</u> it's worth.
7) <u>Don't get distracted</u> by what others are doing.

Dealing with FEPs (Frequent Exam Panics)

 If you can't answer a question...
Move on to the next question and come back to it later.

 If you're running out of time...
Answer questions which require short answers to pick up as many marks as possible.

 If you realise halfway through a question that you've got it wrong...
Cross out what you've done and write your new answer beneath it.

 If you realise that cake you left on the side is at the mercy of your sibling...
Silently bid farewell to your lost dessert and then refocus on the exam.

After the Exam

Whether it's the first exam or the fifteenth, and whether you think it went well or not, congratulate yourself on getting a step closer to the end. All that's left to know is what to do after you step out of that exam hall.

Worrying Won't Change Anything

1) You might find it <u>stressful</u> to <u>talk to friends</u> about the exam — <u>it's okay</u> if you don't want to.

2) Try not to worry about <u>your answers</u> — you <u>can't change</u> what you wrote in the exam.

3) <u>Learn</u> from the experience for <u>future exams</u>. For example:

> If you <u>ran out of time</u>, think about how you could <u>manage</u> your time <u>differently</u>.

> If you <u>felt tired</u>, consider how to improve your routine <u>the night before</u>.

Take Some Time Out to Relax

1) Exams are tiring — try to <u>relax</u> after the exam or do <u>something fun</u>.

2) If you're feeling frustrated or anxious, doing some <u>exercise</u> could help.

3) If you have another exam later <u>the same day</u> or <u>the next day</u>:

- You may want to have a quick look over <u>some notes</u>.
- But be sure to <u>have a break</u> between looking at any notes and the exam.
- <u>Don't forget any final preparations</u> for the next exam (see p.43).

4) <u>And finally...</u>

BE PROUD THAT YOU'VE TICKED AN EXAM OFF YOUR LIST!

~~Scream and Dance Around~~ Unwind After Your Last Exam

1) When all your exams are over, store your revision notes <u>out of sight</u> (but don't throw them away).

2) <u>Celebrate</u> your hard work — have a nice dinner, go on a trip or spend time with friends.

To fill the revision-shaped hole in my life, I memorised cereal ingredients...

Try to put exams to the back of your mind and not worry about results day. Enjoy the well-earned free time you have, maybe by learning a new party trick — wholegrain wheat, sugar, barley, salt, iron, vitamin B6...

Make A Revision Timetable

The last part of this book is a revision planner (all paper-based I'm afraid — we had a bit of a struggle finding a personal assistant who would fit). It'll help you get organised and as ready as can be for all your revision.

Your revision planner and timetable can be found on pages 52-85 of this book. There are spaces for you to fill in all of your exams, other commitments and planned revision sessions.

1) Write Down when all your Exams are

- The first step is to fill in the Exam Timetable on page 52.
- You should refer to this regularly, so you can see at-a-glance which exams you've got coming up. It'll help you stay focused.

EXAMPLE:

Exam Timetable

Subject	Paper	Date	Time
Maths	Paper 1 (non calc)	May 15th (Mon)	9:00
Biology	Paper 1	May 17th (Wed)	14:00
French	Reading	May 22nd (Mon)	14:00
French	Listening	May 23rd (Tues)	9:00
Biology	Paper 2	May 26th (Fri)	9:00

2) Break each Subject Down into Topics

- Fill in the Topic Planners on pages 53-67 for each of your subjects (see below).
- Look at the exam board specification for each subject to find a list of topics, or ask your teachers.
- Put a tick in the correct column to show how happy you are with each topic. Throughout your revision, update the table as you feel more confident.
- Make sure you do enough revision and practice so that you're happy with each topic.

Don't worry if you're unsure about a lot of your topics at first. The whole point of revision is that you get more confident as you go on.

EXAMPLE:

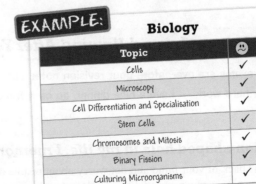

Biology

Topic	☹	😐	😊
Cells	✓		
Microscopy	✓		
Cell Differentiation and Specialisation	✓	✓	
Stem Cells	✓		
Chromosomes and Mitosis	✓		
Binary Fission	✓	✓	
Culturing Microorganisms	✓		

Your Revision Timetable

Make A Revision Timetable

- Write down all your <u>exams</u> in the correct days on your <u>timetable</u>.
- Start from the <u>end</u> — write down your <u>last exam</u> on the <u>last page</u> of the timetable, then <u>work backwards</u>, filling in the dates and other exams until you get to your <u>first exam</u>.

EXAMPLE:

Say your last exam is French Speaking, on the morning of Wednesday 28th June. You'd follow the instructions shown below, in the correct order.

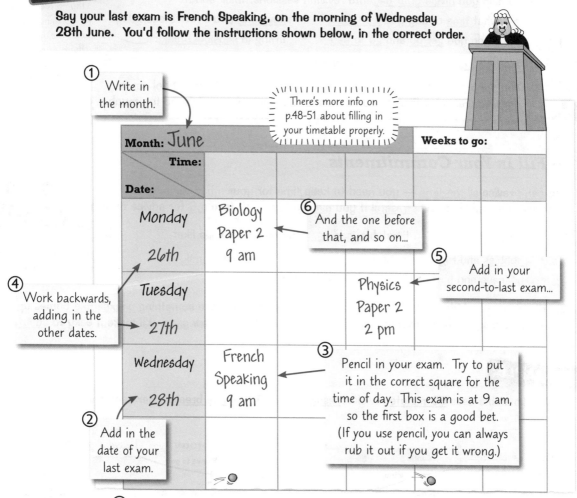

① Write in the month.

There's more info on p.48-51 about filling in your timetable properly.

Month: June	Time:			Weeks to go:
Date:				
Monday 26th	Biology Paper 2 9 am			
Tuesday 27th			Physics Paper 2 2 pm	
Wednesday 28th	French Speaking 9 am			

④ Work backwards, adding in the other dates.

⑥ And the one before that, and so on...

⑤ Add in your second-to-last exam...

③ Pencil in your exam. Try to put it in the correct square for the time of day. This exam is at 9 am, so the first box is a good bet. (If you use pencil, you can always rub it out if you get it wrong.)

② Add in the date of your last exam.

⑦ Once you've done the last page, move to the previous page. Carefully working backwards, fill in all the dates next to Sun, Sat, Fri etc.

Continue backwards, dating the pages until you get to the date you're starting your revision. (Just make sure you use the correct number of days for each month.)

Make A Revision Timetable

It might seem like a lot of organisation that isn't getting any of the subject stuff in your head, but good planning now will save all sorts of time later — time that can be spent, y'know, revising.

4) Divide Your Time Into Sessions

1) The revision timetables in this book are split into <u>five sessions</u> — the <u>time spaces</u> have been left blank so that you can <u>choose them yourself</u>.

2) To help you <u>divide your day</u> into revision sessions, think about:
- what <u>time</u> of day you <u>work best</u>
- <u>how long</u> you'll revise each day
- when you <u>get up</u> and <u>go to bed</u>
- fitting in <u>sensible breaks</u>

3) It's <u>up to you how long</u> each session is.

4) You <u>don't need</u> to use <u>every session each day</u> — you'll be in school some days so cramming five revision sessions into the evening might be too much.

A good rule of thumb is to break for 10 minutes every hour — either in one chunk, or split into two 5-minute breaks.

5) Fill In Your Commitments

You <u>can't</u> revise <u>all the time</u> — you need to keep time for your <u>other commitments</u>. Your revision could become <u>stressful</u> if you <u>overload yourself</u> (see <u>p.6</u> for advice on this).

1) <u>Go through</u> your revision timetable, <u>adding in</u> the time for things like:
- <u>hobbies</u> and regular <u>exercise</u>
- time with <u>friends</u> and <u>family</u>
- <u>holidays</u> and <u>birthdays</u>
- part-time <u>jobs</u>

You may need to cut back on some though — revision is still your priority.

2) It's also a good idea to <u>keep some time free</u> in your plan in case something <u>unexpected</u> comes up — there may be things that you can't plan for, so if there's a few <u>gaps</u>, it'll make it easy to <u>adapt</u>.

EXAMPLE:

This timetable uses <u>50-minute</u> revision <u>sessions</u>, with <u>10-minute breaks</u> after each one.

<u>Start</u> at a <u>sensible time</u>, based on your daily routine.

Leave a <u>gap</u> for <u>lunch</u>.

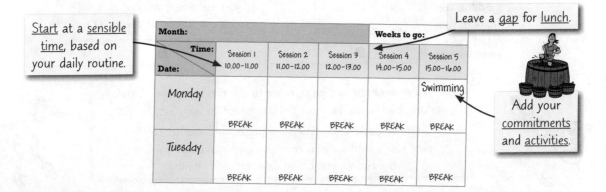

Month:				Weeks to go:	
Time:	Session 1	Session 2	Session 3	Session 4	Session 5
Date:	10.00–11.00	11.00–12.00	12.00–13.00	14.00–15.00	15.00–16.00
Monday					Swimming
	BREAK	BREAK	BREAK	BREAK	BREAK
Tuesday					
	BREAK	BREAK	BREAK	BREAK	BREAK

Add your <u>commitments</u> and <u>activities</u>.

Make A Revision Timetable

6) Add Your Subjects

1) Decide <u>how much time</u> you'll need to spend on each subject by thinking about:
   - which you find the <u>hardest</u>
   - which have <u>more content</u>
   - which you will be <u>examined on first</u>

2) <u>Add your subjects</u> into the timetable, <u>working backwards</u> from the exam.

3) Make sure you allow enough time for each and <u>space them out</u> over the time you have (<u>see p.50</u> for more on this).

> Colour-coding your timetable by subject makes it clearer.

EXAMPLE:

Month:	Time:	Session 1 10.00–11.00	Session 2 11.00–12.00	Session 3 12.00–13.00	Session 4 14.00–15.00	Session 5 15.00–16.00	Weeks to go:
Monday		Biology	French	Maths	History	Swimming	
		BREAK	BREAK	BREAK	BREAK	BREAK	
Tuesday		English Lit	Geography	Biology	French	History	
		BREAK	BREAK	BREAK	BREAK	BREAK	

7) Add Your Topics

1) For each subject, look at the <u>topics</u> in your <u>topic planner</u> — think about which you should <u>prioritise</u> (like you did with your subjects) and <u>add those first</u>.

2) Aim to include <u>topics multiple times</u> to give you a chance to revise them <u>thoroughly</u> and more <u>concisely</u> each time, e.g. by using a range of the <u>techniques</u> covered in Section 2 (<u>p.9-20</u>).

3) Make sure you <u>leave</u> plenty of <u>space</u> for all your topics — you might want to write in <u>pencil</u> to start with.

You <u>don't have to</u> do this step <u>straight away</u> — you might prefer to fill in the topics at the <u>start of each week</u> once you know how you're getting on. Don't be afraid to <u>edit your timetable</u> as you go along, depending on what's going well and what you feel less confident with. Just make sure you leave <u>enough time</u> to cover <u>every topic</u> in enough <u>detail</u>.

EXAMPLE:

Month:	Time:	Session 1 10.00–11.00	Session 2 11.00–12.00	Session 3 12.00–13.00	Session 4 14.00–15.00	Session 5 15.00–16.00	Weeks to go:
Monday		Biology -Cell Biology	French -Speaking Practice	Maths -Algebra	History -The Great Depression	Swimming	
		BREAK	BREAK	BREAK	BREAK	BREAK	
Tuesday		English -Poetry	Geography -Tropical Rainforests	Biology -Infection and Response	French -Past tenses	History -Elizabeth I	
		BREAK	BREAK	BREAK	BREAK	BREAK	

> Add <u>topic detail</u> under each subject.

Space It Out and Mix It Up

Think About S p a c i n g As You Plan Your Revision

Revisiting a topic several times, with gaps in between, is more effective than trying to revise it all in one go. It helps the information sink in better so that it's easier to remember in the exam.

① Space out your revision for a topic across the time you have available — make sure you leave enough time to go over a topic more than once.

② Don't be tempted to cram a whole subject into a day — your revision won't be as effective.

③ It's okay to cover different topics from the same subject on the same day, just make sure you don't do it too often — keep your revision varied to keep your brain engaged.

Make Sure You Mix Your Subjects Up

1) Include a good mix of subjects every day — don't cover all your languages or sciences in one go.

2) Split your revision of each subject into short, focused chunks spread over different days and several weeks — leaving a gap between them will help you retain the information better.

3) It's not a good idea to spend a week revising just Maths and then a week on English — the information just won't stay in your brain in the long-term.

> This example spaces subjects out well and mixes them up, with regular gaps in between. You'd just need to add in your topics and short breaks...

EXAMPLE:

Month: Date \ Time	Session 1 10.00–11.00	Session 2 11.00–12.00	Session 3 12.00–13.00	Session 4 14.00–15.00	Session 5 15.00–16.00	Weeks to go:
Monday	Biology	French	Maths	History	Swimming	
Tuesday	English Lit	Geography	Biology	French	History	
Wednesday	Maths	Run with Dad	Spanish	English Lit	Physics	
Thursday	←	Trip to town	→	Chemistry	History	
Friday	French	English Lit	Physics	English Lang	Maths	
Saturday	History	Swimming	Spanish	Chemistry	Physics	
Sunday	Tennis	Chemistry	English Lang	Spanish	English Lit	

My timetables are so good, people call me a revisionary...

Oh come on, that was a good one. Speaking of good ones, you should have a pretty gosh darn good timetable in front of you by this point. Just a couple more things before you go...

Checking Your Revision Timetable

Hey, you, I see you about to skip this page — before you race off excitedly to start using your shiny new timetable, it's a good idea to spend a few minutes checking you haven't .... anything important.

Check Your Timetable

1) Run through the <u>checklist</u> below and compare each point with your timetable.
2) If there's <u>anything missing</u>, go back and <u>fill it in</u>.

1. Have you included <u>all your exams</u> for every subject? ☑

2. Have you added in <u>topics</u> for at least the first few weeks? ☑

3. Have you double-checked the <u>dates</u>? ☑

4. Does the timetable cover a <u>mixture of subjects</u> each day? ☑

5. Have you planned in <u>regular breaks</u>? ☑

6. Have you left time for <u>things you enjoy</u> doing? ☑

7. Have you left a few <u>gaps</u> to change things if you need to? ☑

Stick To Your Timetable — but be Flexible

It's all well and good making yourself a great timetable, but it's no use to you unless you <u>follow it</u>.

1) Use your <u>revision timetable</u> alongside your <u>topic planners</u> to keep track of your <u>progress</u>.

2) Don't be afraid to <u>adapt</u> the plan as you go — if you know your German tense endings better than you thought but need to spend more time on quadratic equations, just <u>swap things around</u> as you need to.

3) If something doesn't go to plan one day, <u>don't panic</u> — just fit any <u>missed revision</u> into the <u>gaps</u> you've left in the timetable and <u>carry on</u>.

Exam Timetable

Subject	Paper	Date	Time

Subject: Maths

Topic	🙁	😐	🙂
Multiples, Factors & Primes			
Fractions			
Decimals			
Percentages			
Rounding & Estimating			
Powers & Roots			
Multiplying out brackets			
Factorising			
Surds			

Subject: _____

Topic	😟	🙂	😃

Subject: _____

Topic	🙁	🙂	😉

Subject: _____

Topic	😖	🙂	😉

Your Revision Timetable

Subject: _____

Topic	😟	🙂	😃

Subject: _____

Topic	🙁	🙂	😉

Subject: _____

Topic	😟	😐	😉

Subject: _____

Topic	☹	🙂	😉

Subject: _____

Topic	😐	🙂	😉

Subject: _____

Topic	☹	☺	😉

Subject: _____

Topic	😖	🙂	😉

Subject: _____

Topic	😣	🙂	😄

Subject: _____

Topic	😕	🙂	😉

Your Revision Timetable

Subject: _____

Topic	😟	🙂	😉

Your Revision Timetable

Subject: _____

Topic	😣	🙂	😉

Your Revision Timetable

Revision Timetable

See p.49 for an example of a completed timetable.

Month:				Weeks to go:	
Time: / Date:					
Monday					
Tuesday					
Wednesday					
Thursday					
Friday					
Saturday					
Sunday					

Revision Timetable

Month:				Weeks to go:	
Time: / Date:					
Monday					
Tuesday					
Wednesday					
Thursday					
Friday					
Saturday					
Sunday					

Your Revision Timetable

Revision Timetable

Month:				Weeks to go:	
Time: Date:					
Monday					
Tuesday					
Wednesday					
Thursday					
Friday					
Saturday					
Sunday					

Revision Timetable

Month:				Weeks to go:	
Time: Date:					
Monday					
Tuesday					
Wednesday					
Thursday					
Friday					
Saturday					
Sunday					

Revision Timetable

Month:				Weeks to go:	
Time: **Date:**					
Monday					
Tuesday					
Wednesday					
Thursday					
Friday					
Saturday					
Sunday					

Revision Timetable

Month:				Weeks to go:
Time: / Date:				
Monday				
Tuesday				
Wednesday				
Thursday				
Friday				
Saturday				
Sunday				

Revision Timetable

Month:					Weeks to go:	
Time: **Date:**						
Monday						
Tuesday						
Wednesday						
Thursday						
Friday						
Saturday						
Sunday						

'How to waste your Revision Timetable

Month: Joooooone		**Weeks to go:** 6	

FINISH WEEK 6 TIMETABLE

Date: \ Time:	10-11		2-3	3-4
Monday				(Procrasti-)baking — brownies?
Tuesday	Tidy room (again)	Write a haiku about Maths revision		
Wednesday			Sort clothes into colour order	Sort clothes into length order
Thursday				
Friday		Put books in alphabetical order by the second letter of the third chapter	Stare at Spanish verbs until enough time has passed to get another snack	
Saturday	Watch the shopping channel			
Sunday		Learn how to line dance		

How not to fill in Your Revision Timetable

Revision Timetable

Month:				Weeks to go:	
Time: / Date:					
Monday					
Tuesday					
Wednesday					
Thursday					
Friday					
Saturday					
Sunday					

Revision Timetable

Month:				Weeks to go:	
Time: / Date:					
Monday					
Tuesday					
Wednesday					
Thursday					
Friday					
Saturday					
Sunday					

Revision Timetable

Month:				Weeks to go:	
Time: Date:					
Monday					
Tuesday					
Wednesday					
Thursday					
Friday					
Saturday					
Sunday					

Your Revision Timetable

Revision Timetable

Month:				Weeks to go:	
Time: / **Date:**					
Monday					
Tuesday					
Wednesday					
Thursday					
Friday					
Saturday					
Sunday					

Your Revision Timetable

Revision Timetable

Month:				Weeks to go:	
Time: **Date:**					
Monday					
Tuesday					
Wednesday					
Thursday					
Friday					
Saturday					
Sunday					

Revision Timetable

Month:				Weeks to go:	
Time: Date:					
Monday					
Tuesday					
Wednesday					
Thursday					
Friday					
Saturday					
Sunday					

Revision Timetable

Month:				Weeks to go:	
Time: / **Date:**					
Monday					
Tuesday					
Wednesday					
Thursday					
Friday					
Saturday					
Sunday					

Your Revision Timetable

Revision Timetable

Month:				Weeks to go:	
Time: **Date:**					
Monday					
Tuesday					
Wednesday					
Thursday					
Friday					
Saturday					
Sunday					

Revision Timetable

Month:				Weeks to go:	
Time: / **Date:**					
Monday					
Tuesday					
Wednesday					
Thursday					
Friday					
Saturday					
Sunday					

Revision Timetable

Month:				Weeks to go:	
Time: **Date:**					
Monday					
Tuesday					
Wednesday					
Thursday					
Friday					
Saturday					
Sunday					

Top 10 Ultimate Revision Tips

Here are the absolute must-know, save-your-life-in-a-fight-with-a-zombie-exam-paper, ultimate revision tips.

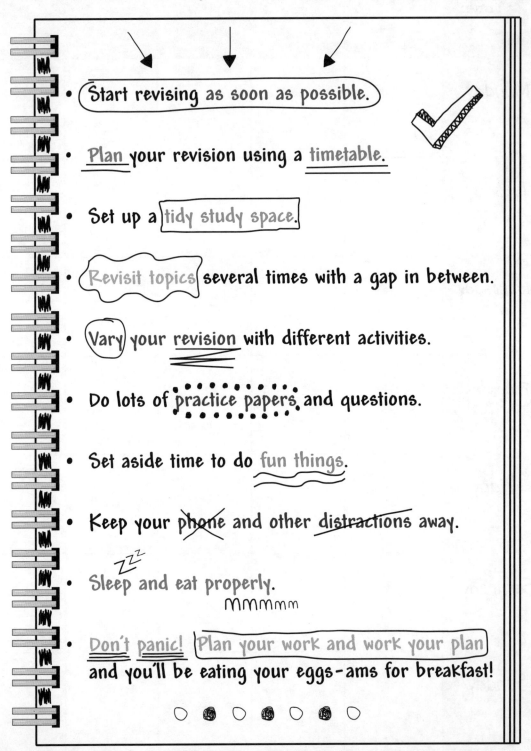

- Start revising as soon as possible.

- Plan your revision using a timetable.

- Set up a tidy study space.

- Revisit topics several times with a gap in between.

- Vary your revision with different activities.

- Do lots of practice papers and questions.

- Set aside time to do fun things.

- Keep your phone and other distractions away.

- Sleep and eat properly.

- Don't panic! Plan your work and work your plan and you'll be eating your eggs-ams for breakfast!